THIS NEW NOISE

THE EXTRAORDINARY BIRTH AND
TROUBLED LIFE OF THE BBC

Charlotte Higgins

First published 2015
by Guardian Books, Kings Place, 90 York Way, London, N1 9GU
and Faber & Faber Ltd, Bloomsbury House,
74-77 Great Russell Street, London, WC1B 3DA

The right of Charlotte Higgins to be identified as the author of this work
has been asserted in accordance with Section 77 of the Copyright,
Designs and Patents Act 1988

Text design by Faber
Printed and bound by CPI Group (UK) Ltd, Croydon CR0 4YY

A CIP record for this book
is available from the British Library
ISBN 978-1-78335-072-8

2 4 6 8 10 9 7 5 3 1

In memoriam
Georgina Henry
1960–2014

'Wireless', a term that has far too recently entered our vocabulary, a term whose success has been far too swift for it not to have carried with it a good many of our era's dreams and for it not to have provided me with one of those rare and specifically modern measures of our mind. It is faint gauges of this sort that occasionally give me the illusion that I am embarked on some great adventure, that I somewhat resemble a seeker of gold: the gold I seek is in the air.

> André Breton, *Introduction to the Discourse on the Paucity of Reality* (1924), translated by Richard Sieburth and Jennifer Gordon

The BBC came to pass silently, invisibly; like a coral reef, cells busily multiplying, until it was a vast structure, a conglomeration of studios, offices, cool passages along which many passed to and fro; a society, with its king and lords and commoners, its laws and dossiers and revenue and easily suppressed insurrection . . .

> Malcolm Muggeridge, *The Thirties* (1940)

Contents

x

Introduction

The BBC is an institution at the heart of Britain. The BBC defines and expresses Britishness – to those who live in the UK, and to the rest of the world. The BBC, to my mind at least, is the most powerful British institution of them all, for, as well as informing, educating and entertaining, it permeates and reflects our existences, infiltrates our imaginations, forms us in myriad ways. It seeps into us. It is the stuff of our inner lives.

Unlike, say, the monarchy, or the armed forces, the BBC is an institution that is still young. As I write there are still those alive who can remember a time before the wireless. And yet in so many ways the age that birthed the BBC – that of modernism and the rise of mechanisation – can seem completely out of reach, as alien to us now as the ancient world. The years that separate us from its formation have been years of rapid change: the mass production of antibiotics, the Second World War, the atom bomb, the contraceptive pill, the Internet, 9/11, the rise of China . . . Perhaps, though, the threshold on which we stand now, hovering irresolute as we do between the analogue and digital eras, is not so different from the frightening and exciting changes wrought by modernism. The body politic, then as now, had a series of important choices to make about how to incorporate epoch-defining technological advances into the lives of the citizenry.

This book comes out of an unusual journalistic assignment. Alan Rusbridger, the editor of the *Guardian*, asked me to suspend my normal work as chief arts writer, and spend 'several months' researching the BBC. The fruits of this enterprise would be a series of long essays for the paper, and this book. The notion was to try to deepen the debate about the broadcaster, which had often been shrill and bad tempered. Alan asked me to try to get under the skin of the institution. Cheerfully, he informed me it was the biggest single assignment he had ever commissioned.

'Several months' turned into a year. The scale of the organisation alone (at the time it had 21,000 employees) and the range of its work made the task immense. Trying to understand the BBC is like trying to understand a city-state. It has its court, its grandees and aristocrats, its artists and creators, its put-upon working class, its cliques and dissidents and rebels, its hangers-on and corrupters and criminals. It has its folklore and mythology, its customs and rituals.

Over my year with the BBC, I spent (or so it seemed) more time in the BBC's various offices than in the *Guardian*'s. I conducted over a hundred long interviews with employees and those who knew the corporation well, from secretaries to directors general. I became convinced that to understand the BBC it was necessary to delve into its past, and so I absorbed as much as I could of the huge literature on the BBC, starting with Asa Briggs's multivolume history of British broadcasting. Towards the end of the project, I also spent time in the BBC's Written Archives. It became clear to me that many of the qualities of the BBC are still dependent on the way it was first shaped. As one BBC journalist said to me, 'Reith still stalks the corridors.' Concomitantly, many of its recent problems have been foreshadowed and prefigured. The aim was not to present a linear history of the BBC but to offer a picture of the corporation as I encountered it over that year, deepened and enriched by the soundings I would take in the deep waters of its past.

In October 2013, when I began the assignment, the BBC felt fragile and insecure after the travails of the recent past. Less than a year earlier, George Entwistle, the director general, had resigned after only 54 days in post, as a result of two closely connected scandals. These were the handling by the current affairs programme *Newsnight* of allegations into sexual abuse by the BBC's one-time star, Jimmy Savile; and the incorrect naming on the Internet, after an investigation by the same programme, of an innocent man as a paedophile. The BBC Trust's chairman, Lord Patten, had also come under enormous pressure, and would resign through ill-health partway through my work on the BBC, in spring 2014. The BBC's huge pay-offs to former managers were also under public scrutiny, and the corporation was being severely criticised for an abandoned technology project, the Digital Media Initiative, which had cost £100 million. No day passed, it seemed, without hostile headlines, the enmity of elements of the press fuelled by commercial rivalry.

There was perhaps even a greater existential threat. The BBC now operates in an era of unprecedented media fragmentation. We live in a world of Netflix and YouTube, of Google, Amazon and Apple – a world in which anyone can be a broadcaster, a world where the sheer bulk of encroaching global media businesses threatens the corporation. In my childhood the BBC was grandly dominant, standing out on the horizon like a great cathedral on a plain; only ITV and, later, Channel 4 were also visible in the landscape. Now that plain was built over and populous; great edifices loomed above the BBC, and threatened to cast it wholly into shadow. The very funding mechanism of the licence fee – a levy on television ownership – was beginning to look outmoded and shaky in the world of catch-up, the tablet and the smartphone. Politicians, for the most part, seemed indifferent or hostile, especially on the right. Urgent questions presented themselves: were we, as a nation, drifting towards squandering the inheritance of the BBC through sheer carelessness? Was the BBC worth fighting for? Had it grown too unwieldy and too powerful, as its detractors claimed? With its vast and tentacular commercial operations, was it trampling its smaller rivals? Was it succeeding in its basic and founding aims of impartiality and independence? It was with such questions in mind that I entered the great citadel of the BBC.

PART ONE

ORIGINS AND ARCHITECTS

1

Reith of the BBC

The manse on Lynedoch Street, Glasgow, is a handsome double-fronted house with nine steps up to its front door. It clings to the flank of its sandstone church, whose brace of tall, pencil-straight towers are linked by an elegant classical pediment. The manse – which still exhales an air of four-square Victorian respectability – occupies the high ground above the wide green spaces of Kelvingrove Park, in which, before the First World War, its son John Reith would walk, feeling the winds of destiny brushing his cheek as they blew down from the Campsie Fells – or so he said. Even when a teenager, Reith, all six foot six of him, had a face with something of the Easter Island carving about it: graven, austere, immense jawed. As he aged, the dark bushy eyebrows became more wayward and independently active, the white hair wilder. There is footage of him being interviewed in 1967 by Malcolm Muggeridge. When the terrifying, wolfish smile comes, the face looks as if it has been hacked open with a hammer and chisel.

The church has now been converted into the premises of an accountancy firm and a business consultancy, which would horrify the intensely religious Reith: in his youth it resounded to sermons given by his father George, a Free Presbyterian minister whom the son worshipped second only to God the Father: 'His sense of grace was apostolic;

his sense of righteousness prophetic,' remembered Reith. 'When he spoke on social or moral ill, or in defence of one whom he felt to be unjustly assailed, his eyes would flash; the eloquence of his indignation was devastating.' The church 'was one of the wealthiest, most influential, most liberal in Scotland'. Its congregation, in the British Empire's prosperous, productive second city, encompassed 'merchant princes, great industrialists, professors' to a 'considerable element of the humble but equally worthy sort – master tradesmen and foremen from shipyards and works . . .' There was also a church mission that reached beyond Reith's well-heeled parish to 'a poor section of the city': this was a self-conscious embrace of the whole social scale.

Reith grew up in an atmosphere of rigid piety. His parents were distant idols, seen only at mealtimes. At school, he did not flourish; he was removed from the Glasgow Academy after bullying two classmates, and sent to board at Gresham's in Norfolk, where, eventually, he did better. But, to his bitter regret, his academic record was considered insufficient for university, and his father, calling him into his study one day, announced that he should follow a trade. He was duly apprenticed at an engineering firm. When war broke out in 1914, he joined up, and proved himself a bloody-minded and occasionally insubordinate soldier. One morning in France in 1915, when he was out inspecting a damaged communications trench, his tall and conspicuous figure was found to be a convenient target for a sniper. Part of the left side of his face was shot off, leaving a jagged scar. Relieved thereafter from active

John Reith. 'He would look through you . . . like a dowager
duchess meeting a chimney sweep.'

service, he spent happy and productive months in America as an inspector of small arms being produced for the
war effort.

By the autumn of 1922, Reith was unexactingly
employed as honorary secretary to the Conservative politician Sir William Bull. According to the account in Reith's
autobiography, on 13 October, while scouring the newspapers, an advertisement caught his eye in the situations-
vacant column. It read: 'The British Broadcasting Company
(in formation). Applications are invited for the following
officers: General Manager, Director of Programmes, Chief
Engineer, Secretary. Only applicants having first-class
qualifications need apply. Applications to be addressed to
Sir William Noble, Chairman of the Broadcasting Committee, Magnet House, Kingsway, WC2.' Reith wrote an
application and dropped it into his club's post box – then
thought to read Noble's entry in *Who's Who*, and fished

out his letter, rewriting it to emphasise his Aberdonian ancestry in an attempt to appeal to his putative employer's local loyalties. His interview consisted of 'a few superficial questions', he recalled in his memoir, *Into the Wind*. He added: 'I did not know what broadcasting was.' Many might have quailed in the face of their own ignorance, but not Reith. Not long before, having listened to an especially energising sermon at the Presbyterian church in Regent Square, Bloomsbury, he had written in his diary, 'I still believe there is some great work for me to do in the world.'

He was duly appointed general manager, and for the next few days, still in utter ignorance of what his new job might be, tried to 'bring every casual conversation round to "broadcasting"' until an acquaintance enlightened him. On 22 December 1922 he turned up at the offices (deserted, as it was a Saturday). He found 'a room about 30 foot by 15, furnished with three long tables and some chairs. A door at one end invited examination; a tiny compartment six foot square; here a table and a chair; also a telephone. "This", I thought, "is the general manager's office."' ('Little more than a cupboard,' remembered Peter Eckersley, the BBC's first chief engineer.) Including Reith, there were four members of staff.

The BBC today, with its workforce of 21,000 and its income of £5 billion, is such an ineluctable part of British national life that it is hard to imagine its birth pangs, comparatively recent as they are. The birth of the BBC outstrips my own parents' lifetimes by only a decade: for them, television was a novelty that became an affordable part of everyday life only in their adulthoods. (One of my father's most vivid early memories was the announcement on the wireless from Neville Chamberlain, on 3 September 1939, that 'This country is at war with Germany' – 'followed shortly afterwards by the air-raid sirens and sitting in the pantry under the stairs waiting for the onslaught', which, disappointingly for a seven-year-old, did not materialise.) The BBC's sounds, its magical moving pictures, its words are not just 'content', as the belittling word of our time has it, but the tissue of our dreams, the warp and weft of our memories, the staging posts of our lives. The BBC is a portal to other worlds, our own time machine; it brings the dead to life. With it we can range across the earth; we can dive to the depths of the ocean; take flight. Once a kindly auntie's voice in the corner of the room, it is now the daemonic voice in our ear, a loving companion from which we need never be parted. It is our playmate, our instructor, our friend. Unlike Google and Amazon, which soothe us by presenting us with the past (their profferings predicated on our web 'history'), the BBC brings us ideas of which we have not yet dreamed, in a space free from the hectoring voices of those who would sell us goods. It tells seafarers when the gales will gust over Malin, Hebrides, Bailey. It brings us the news, and tries to tell it truthfully without fear or favour. It keeps company with the lonely; it brings succour to the isolated. Proverbially, when the bombs rain down, the captain of the last nuclear submarine will judge Britain ended when Radio 4 ceases to sound.

The year the BBC was born was also the year Northern Ireland seceded from the Free State; it was the year James Joyce's *Ulysses* was published; and its creation was sandwiched between the first general election in which women voted (1918) and universal suffrage (1928). Born in the wake of calamitous war, in the high noon of empire, and at the moment of the formation of the United Kingdom as we know it, it took its place as a projection of, and a power in, new ideas about nationhood, modernity and democracy. With the coming of the BBC, it became possible for the first time in these islands' history for a geographically dispersed 'general public' to be able to experience the same events simultaneously – and together to gain what had hitherto been privileged access to the most powerful voices of the land.

This sense of collective experience, so familiar now, was striking and strange at its birth. Malcolm Muggeridge, in his book *The Thirties* (1940), tried to express the novel sense of the BBC thus: 'From nine million wireless sets in nine million homes its voice is heard nightly, giving information, news, entertaining and instructing, preaching even, with different accents yet always the same; the voices of the nine million who listen merged into one voice, their own collective voice echoing back to them.' He also marvelled, darkly, at the gulf between the nature of the news the wireless brought from the world outside – all delivered in reasonable, calm BBC tones – into the haven of the home. One thing came after another, spooling out of the wireless in an endless, undifferentiated stream of sound-matter. 'Comfortable in armchairs, drowsing perhaps, snug and secure, the whole world was available, its tumult compressed into a radio set's small compass. Wars and rumours of wars, all the misery and passion of a troubled world, thus came into their consciousness, in winter with curtains drawn and a cheerful fire blazing; in summer often out of doors, sprawling on a lawn or under a tree, or in a motorcar, indolently listening while telegraph poles flashed past. Dollfuss had been murdered, despairing Jews had resorted to gas ovens . . . and the king and queen had received a warm welcome in Hackney – well, there it was, and now for another station . . .'

Reith recognised one of the most fundamental qualities of broadcasting: it is superabundant. It knows no scarcity; it cannot run out: 'It does not matter how many thousands there may be listening; there is always enough for others', as he put it in his 1924 book *Broadcast Over Britain*. 'It is a reversal of the natural law, that the more one takes, the less there is for others . . . There is no limit to the amount that may be drawn off.' And because everyone can have as much as they like of it, broadcasting, at least as delivered by the fledgling BBC, is no respecter of persons; it is the same for everyone: 'Most of the good things of this world are badly distributed and most people have to go without them. Wireless is a good thing, but it may be shared by all alike, for the same outlay, and to the same extent . . . The genius and the fool, the wealthy and the poor listen simultaneously . . . there is no first and third class.' Broadcasting, said Reith, had the effect of 'making the nation as one man'. It was Reith who attached this Arnoldian, culturally unifying ideology to the idea of broadcasting. This ideology, despite the optimism of American broadcasting pioneers such as the engineer David Sarnoff, who in June 1922 wrote of wireless's function as 'entertaining, informing and educating the nation', was lacking in the United States, which was in the grip of a wireless craze by the mid-1920s. There, a cacophony of competing commercial stations grew up, strung between coast and coast. By 1925 there were 5.5 million American wireless sets and 346 stations.

That the BBC should have been set up as a company and a monopoly, and then a corporation in the public interest, was not inevitable, but the result of a series of incremental decisions at first pragmatic and then solidified into ideology. And before broadcasting was armoured in Reithian principles, it was first a technology. In the village of Pontecchio Marconi, a few kilometres south of Bologna in central Italy, is the remarkable sight of Guglielmo Marconi's mausoleum, a kind of manmade travertine cave hewn into the rolling lawns of the Villa Griffone, the elegant nineteenth-century house he shared with his Scots-Irish wife Annie Jameson, scion of the Jameson whiskey empire. An enthusiastic fascist in later life, Marconi was accorded a state funeral by Mussolini, and his tomb has all the pomp – and distinctive, ruggedly geometric style – associated with the aesthetics of that regime. 'Diede con la scoperta il sigillo a un'epoca della storia umana', declares the epitaph inside the monument, itself a phrase from the speech Mussolini gave after his death. It translates: 'With his discovery he set his mark upon an era of human history.'

In truth, in the way of most scientific discoveries, it was a cluster of advances by a number of researchers that led the way to broadcasting. It was the German Heinrich Hertz who, before he died aged only thirty-six in 1894, demonstrated the existence of electromagnetic waves. In 1902 an American, R. A. Fessenden, used wireless waves to carry the human voice over the distance of a mile. The north Staffordshire-born Oliver Lodge developed a tuning device to control the wavelength of a receiver. There were French, American and Russian discoveries, too, in the years before the First World War. Wireless telegraphy and wireless telephony – sending signals or the voice 'through the ether' without wire or cable – was becoming a reality. Marconi coupled his celebrated transatlantic radio experiments with an eye for commercial opportunities and a talent for business. In 1897, he founded the Marconi Wireless Telegraph and Signal Company. He did so in Britain, because it seemed to him that radio could be commercially exploited as a means of communications to shipping – and Britain was the great marine mercantile nation. Broadcasting – the notion of one voice speaking to many – was not yet recognised as a prospect in view, and certainly not as a virtue of the technology. As Asa Briggs pointed out in the first of his magisterial five volumes on the history of British broadcasting, the notion that radio signals could be heard widely was at first regarded as a 'positive nuisance', a hindrance to what was regarded as wireless's most likely application in point-to-point communication. Briggs quoted Lodge, in a parliamentary select committee report of 1907, making the first small intellectual gropings towards something different – that it might have a purpose for 'reporting races and other sporting events, and generally for all important matters occurring beyond the range of the permanent lines'.

The First World War hastened developments. As the early BBC employee Hilda Matheson wrote in her book *Broadcasting* (1933), 'The Great War . . . gave an impetus to wireless communications, as to other forms of practical science, destructive as well as constructive. Directions could be sent by code, or *en clair*, to troops on land, to ships in distant oceans, to submarines, and to aeroplanes deploying over enemy territory.' It was after the war that the advantages of sending one signal to a multitude of receivers were recognised. Many of those who had been working as wireless engineers for the military slipped into work for companies such as Marconi. But the appetite for broadcasting came from 'the man in the street', recalled Matheson: a community of wireless enthusiasts grew up, at first more excited by the notion that broadcasting could be done at all rather than by what was actually to be communicated. She wrote, 'There was a host of men and boys with a passionate interest in mechanical contrivances – making amateur telephones from tin cans, rigging up improvised magnetic and electrical apparatus, in sheds, basements and attics, wherever they could find undisturbed corners in which to use lathes, batteries and tools in peace . . . from their ranks came much of the persistence and enthusiasm which provided the first public for broadcasting.'

In the meantime, wireless also became a topic of popular interest – an apparently miraculous phenomenon followed in the newspapers with wonderment. Manufacturers of wireless sets, such as Marconi, held licences granted by the Post Office to conduct experimental transmissions. On 15 June 1920 the *Daily Mail* arranged for a recital by Dame Nellie Melba, who travelled down to the Marconi headquarters in Essex and sang for a half-hour, ending with 'God Save the King' via 'Addio' from *La Bohème* – her voice was heard clearly across Europe, and the event was widely reported. For the first time, broadcasting was planted in the British imagination as a medium replete with possibilities for entertainment. But, as these experiments continued, so disquiet in military circles grew. Wavelengths were being commandeered for 'frivolous', non-military use, it was felt. Briggs quoted a letter of complaint: 'A few days ago the pilot of a Vickers Vimy machine ... was crossing the Channel in a thick fog and was trying to obtain weather and landing reports from Lympne. All he could hear was a musical evening.'

A new settlement was needed. The wireless manufacturers' experimental broadcasts were banned, and then, under pressure from the amateurs, allowed to continue under controlled conditions. The postmaster general, in response to a question in parliament about the future of broadcasting in April 1922, responded that 'it would be impossible to have a large number of firms broadcasting. It would result only in a sort of chaos.' Talks between the wireless manufacturers and the Post Office resulted in a scheme whereby the government would license wireless sets. A new British Broadcasting Company – with a monopoly on broadcasting – would finance its operations from a share of the licence fee and of royalties from sales of sets. Thus a funding mechanism for the service was devised, and the problem of the scarcity of wavelengths for civilian use solved. Moreover, the Post Office had followed a pleasing path of least resistance – it had neatly avoided having to provide the service itself. To many, it seemed an eminently sensible arrangement. The *Manchester Guardian*'s leader of 20 October 1922 noted that 'broadcasting is of all industries the one most clearly marked out for monopoly. It is a choice between monopoly and confusion . . . the only alternative to granting privileges and monopoly to private firms is that the State should do the work itself.'

By 1925, when the Crawford Parliamentary Committee on Broadcasting made its recommendations, some of the societal and political implications of the new service were beginning to become apparent. The decision was taken to transform the young British Broadcasting Company into a public corporation. Broadcasting was too significant to be turned over to mere profit-making. 'No company or body constituted on trade lines for the profit, direct or indirect, of those composing it, can be regarded as adequate in view of the broader considerations now beginning to emerge,' it reported. 'We think a public corporation is the most appropriate organisation . . . its status and duties should correspond with those of a public service.' Reith's *Broadcast Over Britain* had already laid out some of the abiding principles of the corporation-to-be. The BBC should be the citizen's 'guide, philosopher and friend', he wrote. Broadcasting, in his hands, was moulded into something that was not merely a kind of pleasing technological curiosity, but a phenomenon with the capacity to ennoble those who used it. It may, he wrote, 'help to show that mankind is a unity and that the mighty heritage, material, moral and spiritual, if meant for the good of any, is meant for the good of all'. Wireless 'ignores the puny and often artificial barriers which have estranged men from their fellows. It will soon take continents in its stride, outstripping the winds; the divisions of oceans, mountain ranges and deserts will be passed unheeded. It will cast a girdle round the earth with bands that are all the stronger because invisible.'

Reith was drawing on Shakespeare: it was Puck in *A Midsummer Night's Dream* who boasted that he could 'put a girdle round the earth'. Reith cast himself as magician – more Prospero than Puck, for certain. I hear too the voice of his distant, adored preacher father in those rolling, ecclesiastical phrases. And Reith the younger was to outdo his father: his own congregation would consist not just of the good people of the West End of Glasgow, but the whole population of the United Kingdom, and all its empire.

2

'People, telephones, alarms, excursions': Hilda Matheson

Savoy Hill, London, the frost-hard January of 1929. The atmosphere in the offices of the BBC is, according to talks assistant Lionel Fielden, 'one third boarding school, one third Chelsea party, one third crusade'. The head of variety, Eric Maschwitz, finds himself killing a rat in one of the dingy corridors one day by 'the simple method of flattening it with a volume of *Who's Who*'. There are studios, if you can call them that – 'just small rooms with distressing echoes', according to Fielden. His fellow talks assistant, Lance Sieveking, who has a 'vivid and sometimes erratic imagination', has framed notices and set them beside each microphone: 'If you sneeze or rustle papers you will deafen thousands!!!' There is a creaking lift, a set of narrow stone stairs. Offices with coal fires. The BBC is partway through its triumphant march, at breakneck speed, from a staff of four in 1922 to a glorious future in the palatial Broadcasting House, where it will move in three years' time.

The BBC is a 'new and exciting dish, sizzling over the fire', according to Fielden. Val Gielgud is reinventing drama for the wireless. Percy Pitt is conducting music of all types, and Maschwitz is lending his debonair personality to variety shows. Reith stalks the corridors – 'this giant with piercing eyes under shaggy eyebrows', as Fielden thinks of him. Reith's chief enforcer and number two is

Vice-Admiral Charles Carpendale, who commanded the cruiser *Donegal* in the war – he tends to speak to Maschwitz as if he were 'a delinquent rating'. The staff are a curious and heterogeneous lot – people 'who, often on account of some awkward versatility, or of some form of fastidiousness, idealism or general restlessness, never settled down to any humdrum profession after the war', according to Hilda Matheson, the BBC's first director of talks.

Miss Matheson's office: today, because of the cold, she is minded to hold her departmental meeting with everyone sitting 'on the floor round my fire which shocks the great who may come in, terribly', she scribbles in a letter. Running the talks department, she presides over an extraordinarily mixed bag of subject-matter, and she must be master of it all – from theatre criticism to economics, from foreign affairs to tips for housewives. An ordinary morning's work sees her wrangling talks on crime and criminals, ante-natal care, readings of poems by Tagore, and discussions on market forces for farmers. 'Oh what a day, such a scramble – people, telephones, alarms and excursions, interviews, meetings,' she exclaims.

In January 1929 she is forty-one years old, with 'ash-gold hair and grey eyes', according to her old Oxford tutor, Lettice Fisher, the economic historian. She has neatly bobbed hair and a clear gaze. She is slender and fit – eleven hours' walking a day in Alpine Savoy is what she likes to do on holiday, and indeed what she will do for a fortnight come the summer. Sieveking and Fielden are her assistants, and the latter has had to come to terms with the curious notion of a female boss. 'I had at first thought that it would be strange, perhaps impossible, to work under a woman,' he remembered. But Matheson 'drew my admiration, respect, and affection almost instantly . . . She was not supremely intelligent or supremely beautiful or supremely chic or supremely anything, she was just one of those people who are made of pure gold all the way through. You could not imagine Hilda panicking about anything, or failing to meet any situation with composure and charm.' Richard Lambert, editor of the *Listener*, remembered her as 'earnest, intelligent, quick, sympathetic and idealistic'.

She might be calm as far as her juniors are concerned, but on 3 January she is feeling particularly overwhelmed by the claims on her attention:

The afternoon was so busy and my tray bulged so much that I began to get rattled and desperate and to think I couldn't cope with all the horrid accumulations – But Miss Barry took things in hand and calmed me down and saw me through – so all was well, but you know it's awful sometimes – the accumulations of anti-vaccinationists and Esperantists and propagandists on every subject and advertisement-mongers and Members of Parliament and pacifist organisations and women's organisations and Empire Marketing Boards and Channel Tunnel promoters and A. J. Cook and Lord Ronaldshay and Indian musicians and infant welfarers . . . a little overwhelming in the mass.

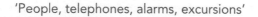

Hilda Matheson: 'earnest, intelligent, quick,
sympathetic and idealistic'

The following day, perhaps thanks to Miss Barry's secre-
tarial efforts, things are more fun, but still wildly busy:
'. . . an interview with and voice test of an Afghan, an intelligent fellow and wise I thought – followed by a similar
process with a charming docker called Bill – a great find

– followed by an hour's discussion with Lionel and a man I have found in the music dept who knows as much about poetry as about music . . .'

In truth, Matheson is struggling to concentrate. Because she is in love – drowning deliciously in it, drugged and drunk with it, utterly brimming with it. She has been in this intoxicated state ever since Monday, 11 December 1928, when Vita Sackville-West, whom she first met the previous summer, came in to the BBC to give a broadcast talk on 'The Modern Woman'. Sackville-West once described the sheer oddness of the new skill of broadcasting in a letter to her husband, Harold Nicolson: 'You are taken into a studio, which is a large and luxuriously appointed room, and there is a desk, heavily padded, and over it hangs a little white box . . . There are lots of menacing notices about "DON'T COUGH – you will deafen millions of people", "DON'T RUSTLE YOUR PAPERS" . . . One has never talked to so few people, or so many; it's very queer.' After the 'Modern Woman' talk, Sackville-West and Matheson spent the night together, and on the Tuesday Matheson stayed off work. On the Wednesday, she wrote to Sackville-West, 'All day – ever since that blessed and ever to be remembered indisposition – I have been thinking of you – bursting with you – and wanting you – oh my god wanting you.'

More than a hundred letters from Matheson to Sackville-West survive, mostly from late December 1928 and the first months of 1929, when Sackville-West was in Berlin with Nicolson, who was serving at the British embassy. Sackville-West's letters are lost – perhaps destroyed

Vita Sackville-West: 'One has never talked to
so few people, or so many.'

by Matheson's family after her death. In her correspondence, Matheson imparts a flesh-and-soul impression of
the triumphs and frustrations of work within the young
BBC. It is an account – knitted tightly into her outpourings
of passion and desire – that dovetails intriguingly with the
trail she left in official memoranda and letters to contributors, as well as in her own published writing. (She
wrote an illuminating work, *Broadcasting*, for the Home
University Library; and was for a time in the 1930s the *Observer*'s wireless critic.) One letter to Sackville-West is written on an official 'internal circulating memo' template,
with its bossy instructions for use: 'Write minutes BELOW
each other and not at all angles – Number your minutes –
Don't write minutes in the margins – ' It is headed 'To:
Orlando. From: Talks director. Subject: Us.' Matheson was

21

referencing Virginia Woolf's novel *Orlando*, which had been published the previous October, and whose gender-shifting hero–heroine was based on Sackville-West. 'I shall write to you on a different office form every day,' she wrote in her speedy, fluidly efficient hand, 'partly to show you the world in which I work, partly to assure myself that it really is me – a filler-in of forms, a writer of memoranda – that you love. Besides I see I shall have to write to you at all sorts of odd moments during the day – covertly in Committees – and this looks so official, nobody would guess.'

That January, Matheson had a momentous project to undertake: organising the first ever broadcast debate between politicians from the three main parties. A ban on 'controversy' in broadcasting had been lifted in 1928, but the BBC was still treading carefully. Endless negotiations were necessary to bring speakers from the Conservative, Liberal and Labour parties together round the microphone to discuss the forthcoming De-rating Bill. (This was legislation, designed to boost the depressed economy, that freed industrial and agricultural premises from local-authority taxation.) On 3 January she wrote of her day, 'Back rather late to find a frenzied Admiral Carpendale sending himself into fits over politics – so I had to draft an ultimatum to the parties for him – rather fun that was.' Later in the day – her letters could stretch over numerous pages, added to at intervals – she becomes the ardent lover again: 'I know that I want you – it engulfs me like a huge wave and I just have to wait till it's passed over my head before I can breathe again . . . sometimes I want you so terribly physically that I can hardly bear it.' Then she switches back to the question of the political debate, telling of a subsequent phone call from Carpendale: 'He's got cold feet because he thought I had rushed him into unseemly and inaccurate letters to the three political parties and I couldn't quite be convincing. Darling, he was so accusing and unfair that I got all hot and bothered . . .'

The following week, on 10 January, the arrangements were still being fought over: 'One final effort to secure my politicians – for the hundredth time of asking – thank heaven they're all fixed now – for the first big political discussion we've yet had . . . they're all as nervous as cats.' The listings deadline for the *Radio Times* had been missed (it is partly for this reason that the politicians who actually spoke are lost to history, though the government spokesman is likely to have been Neville Chamberlain, then health minister, who was behind the bill). The debate, in the end, was 'a great success'. The politicians were 'so very sweet in their passionate desire to be strictly honourable about their allotted time'. Not an impulse, perhaps, that survived long into the broadcast age. The format, too, would surprise current audiences for broadcast political debates. Each speaker was allowed to speak for 20 minutes, with the government spokesman allotted a further 10 minutes at the end. 'It honestly wasn't dull,' promised Matheson. Listeners' letters, she wrote a few days later, were 'pouring in' and they were 'quite amazing'. There was 'a common admission that they hadn't been interested in these things before, but the discussion made them want to know more'.

Matheson, who was born on 7 June 1888, was, like Reith, a child of the manse: her father was a Presbyterian minister in Putney, south London. When she was a teenager he suffered a nervous breakdown, and the family had a spell in Switzerland while he recovered. Matheson was also sent to spend time with families in Stuttgart and Florence. On their return, her father became the first Presbyterian chaplain to students at Oxford, and she studied history as a home student – this in the days before women were officially recognised as members of the university. It was perhaps in Oxford that Matheson made the contacts that led to her recruitment into secret work during the First World War. She was posted to Rome where 'she had the task of forming a proper office on the model of MI5 in London', remembered her mother. Italian officials turned up simply to marvel at her – they were 'very incredulous about the capacity of a young girl, for she did look absurdly young then, to do such work'. (She was twenty-six on the outbreak of war in July 1914.)

After the war, she became political secretary to Nancy Astor, the first woman, in 1919, to take up a seat in the Commons. Astor remembered: 'Those first years in Parliament were only made possible by her unremitting work and service, not for me, but for the cause of women . . . I might describe it as my zeal and her brain.' As part of her work for Astor, Matheson organised a series of receptions where MPs might meet significant women, 'in whom', remembered her mother, 'they had got suddenly interested because they had just got the vote. It was to one of these gatherings she invited Sir John Reith, and he was clever enough to realise that if he could get Hilda, who knew everybody, to come to the BBC he would be doing it a good turn.'

She did indeed know everyone; she was firmly plugged into a network of writers, intellectuals, social reformers and politicians, including some of the most impressively high-flying women of her generation. And if Matheson asked you to broadcast, clearly it was hard to refuse. Her unassailable charm leaps off the page in her letters. One of her greatest catches was H. G. Wells. Various unsuccessful attempts had already been made to get him to the microphone. Matheson tried a new tack: she had a friend of hers, Eileen Power (who was soon to become professor of economic history at the London School of Economics), organise a party at which they would both be present. The morning after it, 14 June 1929, Matheson was in full flow by letter to him – almost flirtatiously berating him for, perhaps, forgetting to give her a lift home (she had to rely on the mercy of philosopher Bertrand Russell, she writes). Then she moves to the kill: 'I have always felt it to be pretty devastating that an internationalist like yourself – perhaps you are the only real internationalist? – shouldn't be making use of the most internationalist means of communication there is.' She goes on to explain that the ban on controversy has been lifted and asks him to go 'on the air' in July. 'It is most awfully important just now, at this moment, that you should say yes, because the stars in their courses are favourable and there is a breath of greater freedom in the world . . . It is fun to address 12 million or so British Islanders and some dozens of millions of

Europeans all in one breath – I do assure you it is. You will be bound to enjoy the full possibilities of broadcasting sooner or later – only why not sooner!'

Wells obediently promises to broadcast on world peace. Power sends Matheson a postcard: 'I'm so glad you snared HG.' He clearly required a deal of looking after. The day before the broadcast she is writing to another contact, Rachel Crowdy, who had been principal commandant of the voluntary nursing operation in the war, and was now heading two sections – one on opium smuggling, another on social reform – at the League of Nations: 'Dear Dame Rachel – This is an absolute SOS . . . could you possibly come and dine with me at 7.30 at the Savoy Grill tomorrow night with H. G. Wells, who is broadcasting at 9.15? This is a remarkable reconciliation, because he has always been a great opponent of broadcasting, and I am sure it will make all the difference if there are one or two people he likes to cheer him up before hand . . . I really do beseech you to say yes.' Also of the party were the Woolfs, Power and Julian Huxley. (Virginia Woolf was no great fan of Matheson. She wrote in her diary that summer of Matheson's 'earnest aspiring competent wooden face . . . A queer trait in Vita – her passion for the earnest middle-class intellectual, however drab & dreary.')

Matheson did not hesitate to draw Sackville-West into her professional dilemmas, consulting 'the big stride of your mind' – and persuading her to do more broadcasting. On 23 January 1929 she is manoeuvring for her lover to become a regular broadcast drama critic. 'I have got the evidence of all the people who say you have got the only decent voice on the wireless of any woman. My own young men I'm not sure of; they will perhaps be amused! However I think I can get away with it quite easily and I should enjoy doing it . . . Oh darling do go on thinking favourably about it – it would be so perfect from my point of view – excuse for your coming to MY OFFICE, benefit untold to my listeners, prestige of the most exalted kind for my BBC. Oh please do.' (The portentous capitals of MY OFFICE are a frequently recurring private jest.) The following week she is asking for Sackville-West's help in suggesting names to contribute to a 'symposium' on modern literature:

> You understand so absolutely about broadcasting and the strangeness of our funny public – bless your heart. It is like you and so clever of you to see that we oughtn't to have a pure Bloomsbury symposium on the novel. Rebecca West is such a devil to deal with and has such a temper, and I don't think she writes good novels, do you? But she is very amusing. Aldous Huxley won't broadcast he says, but of course he might in this series. Clemence Dane has such a nice voice, she might be good, only she has rather hived off to plays. Rose Macaulay? Margaret Kennedy has an annoying voice and manner rather. Well, we must think.

Clemence Dane was the author of *Regiment of Women* and co-wrote the screenplay of *Anna Karenina* starring Greta Garbo; Kennedy was the author of *The Constant Nymph* and *The Ladies of Lyndon*.

One of Matheson's most enduring achievements was her invention of *Week in Westminster*, which still runs on Radio 4 today, and which she began as a programme delivered by women MPs for the benefit of the newly enfranchised female electorate. It had a curious passage to the airwaves. One of Matheson's responsibilities was for household talks. (A reasonably long trail of memoranda in the BBC archives, for example, concerns Matheson's seeking guidance from Reith on whether it is permissible to include recipes for fruit wines in broadcasts, since 'from an economy and food preservative point of view there is much to be said for it'. A note in her handwriting records: 'The DG . . . told me personally that no intoxicants should be included.') At the start of 1929 a series of programmes was broadcast at 10.45 a.m. in collaboration with the Empire Marketing Board. In one of the programmes it was mentioned that listeners could send off for a free recipe sheet. To everyone's surprise, 5,280 requests were made for the leaflet, sufficiently noteworthy for Matheson to write about it to Reith: 'There is nothing at all remarkable about the recipes – various ways of cooking cheese.'

This rudimentary piece of audience research clearly prompted some further thinking. By the summer of that year, she was writing to Megan Lloyd George, David Lloyd George's daughter and, since that May's election, the Liberal MP for Anglesey. Matheson's letter of 10 July began with an outline of the response to the cookery programme and recipe-sheet offer, explaining that she believed there was a 'large public of housewives' who make a practice 'of taking a short pause for a cup of tea in the middle of the morning' to listen to the wireless. This mid-morning slot, usually devoted to household matters, could be given a broader purpose, she suggested. 'It might stimulate a greater interest in Parliament if during the session these weekly talks were given by one or two women Members of Parliament who would give a simple account of the week at Westminster. I believe that this would help perhaps to bring home to listeners that they had a stake in the Government of the country.' It took Matheson several tries to squeeze a 'yes' from Lloyd George. In November she wrote again: 'I am afraid you will think I am a great botherer...' A fortnight later: 'I feel you must think of me as an absolute pest.' Lloyd George finally gave way and began to broadcast – most successfully. The format settled into a pattern: when parliament was sitting, women MPs from the main parties, including Nancy Astor, would speak in weekly rotation. Fielden's memoirs record that, in his view, 'women were (and are) almost never good broadcasters. I don't know why this should be, but it is a fact.' With the single exception, that is, of Lloyd George, whom he rated as 'not only a naturally good broadcaster, but also a person of great charm and gaiety'.

Fielden's certainty about the inferiority of women as broadcasters is a reminder of what Matheson was up against, both as a high-ranking woman within the BBC and as a lesbian. There was no doubt support from her circle of successful women contacts, many of whom came of age during the war. Harold Nicolson thought of her as the very ideal of the competent, ambitious professional woman – his first novel, *Public Faces*, contains a splendid character called Jane Campbell, a superlatively efficient and unruffled parliamentary secretary of foreign affairs, who, he noted in his diary entry of 11 April 1932, was a 'woman . . . of the type of Hilda Matheson'. In the novel, he sketched the character thus: 'a woman of tact, gaiety, and determination . . . a confident woman. She regarded it as quite natural that a person of her attainments . . . should . . . have reached so garish a position'. Campbell 'liked being female: she displayed this liking in every curve of her trim body'. And yet the assumptions at play were greatly alien from those of our own time. In the talk that Sackville-West gave the night she and Matheson became lovers, she had argued (according to the account she gave in a letter to Nicolson) that 'Women *cannot* combine careers with normal life . . . They love too much; they allow love to override everything else. Men don't.'

Sackville-West was underestimating her new lover. Matheson's letters show that love, desire and work mingled seamlessly in her head and heart; but nothing got in the way of her doing her job. Nor was she unduly worried about BBC gossip. She told Sackville-West about the possibility that Fielden was on to them (he is 'as sharp as a ferret and I am told a complete homosexual himself'). But she was, on the whole, defiant: 'I think my position in the BBC and yours in the great world are both far too strong for anyone to do anything to us.' Above all, she was gloriously unashamed of her sexuality. 'What we feel for each other is all good – that as far as I am concerned I know it is part and parcel of anything decent in me – of the best parts of me, not at all of the worst – that it makes more of me, not less . . . I cannot feel one shred of shame or remorse or regret or anything dimly approaching it . . . I loathe the need for furtiveness and secrecy – I find it's incomprehensibly absurd – I have to keep reminding myself that it's considered anti social and immoral – and it makes me fairly blaspheme. There – that's a good explosion.'

Relations between Matheson and Reith gradually began to cool. She was entering bolder and more adventurous territory, and was increasingly falling foul of the director general. In a letter posted on 22 June, and written on BBC headed writing paper, she described in detail to Sackville-West a long 'argument – hammer and tongs – about "controversial subjects" and their treatment' with Reith and the director of programmes, Roger Eckersley. In so doing she laid bare one of the problems of the BBC's principle of impartiality – that it all depends on where you start from: 'He tends to regard as controversial and partisan and therefore inadmissible a talk about which any of his business magnates complain or disapprove, e.g. [critic] Osbert Sitwell, because his on art were objectionable and because all modern art is objectionable and therefore can only be discussed if there is also somebody to put the case for the Victorians or the classics. The fact that *all* talks on art hitherto have been given by spokesmen of the old school and that Osbert, however tiresome, was therefore evening things up, wasn't regarded as relevant.'

Matheson continued: 'What it really amounts to is this – that he only classes or admits as controversial subjects on which he or his friends have views . . . All our sermons are controversial but the DG won't admit it because he agrees with them . . .' The nature of the talks themselves came under discussion: 'They . . . said that all my talks had been getting more and more "educational", and that they were supposed to be "topical" and that talks on current ideas and current topics of speculation or discussion were *not* topical – only talks on *events*, not on problems of the day, like saving the countryside, or the future of the theatre . . .' Matheson detected a suggestion towards what we would now call restructuring of her department. And, in a narrative that many professional women will find depressingly familiar, she remarked, 'They are always so damned ready to say to any *woman* who disagrees with them that it is unreasonable and shows a lack of balance – I do honestly think that . . . afterwards when Roger began to say (a) that they highly valued my work but (b) that I was getting a name for unreasonable truculence I . . . got a choke in my throat which made me so angry and humiliated I couldn't bear it.'

Soon enough she was speculating about whether she would have to resign. In his diary for 6 March 1930, Reith noted that he was 'developing a great dislike of Miss Matheson and her works'. That year, she began working on a series of talks with Nicolson on modern literature. This became a battleground, according to Michael Carney's biography of Matheson. Reith loathed the moderns. A sticking point was whether Nicolson would be allowed to mention the banned texts *Ulysses* and *Lady Chatterley's Lover*. A very BBC fudge was agreed: there was to be no mention of the texts by name but Nicolson was allowed to say that the BBC had forbidden him to mention them. There were other problems. Fielden, in his memoir, perceived that Reith began to regard Matheson as too left wing. 'Gentlemen in the Athenaeum Club were soon whispering to Reith that he was being "run by a Gang of Reds"', he recalled. 'Reith began to turn an enquiring eye upon the talks department, and sent sharp little notes to Hilda suggesting that so and so held eccentric or subversive or atheistic or anarchistic views and was not a suitable person for the microphone . . . the battle was on.'

In December 1931 Matheson finally did resign – a big enough story for the *Manchester Guardian* to cover it two days in a row. (In the edition of 4 December the wireless correspondent noted 'an air of mystery about the resignation of Miss Hilda Matheson . . . it may be taken . . . that differences of opinion have existed for some time at Savoy Hill for some time past between two opposing schools of thought'.) Fielden recalled that nine members of the department threatened to hand in their notice en masse in protest. Lambert later paid her tribute: 'It was Hilda Matheson, toiling single-mindedly night and day, who "made" the talks department a live, energetic and humane department of the corporation.' She had 'provided listeners with an informed criticism of books, films, plays, music and farming, opened up the field of debates and discussions, improved and expanded the news, and sought even to train the politicians to make better use of broadcasting'.

After leaving the BBC, Matheson's next big job was running the Africa Survey for Lord Hailey – a major colonial project that studied the geography, ethnography, economics and politics of the entire continent. Later, in November 1939, her mother remembered, 'a mysterious man began calling her up but would give no name. Finally they met. When she came back from lunching with him, she told me laughingly that he was a man who seemingly knew everything she had done all her life.' Once again, Matheson was being recruited into secret work, this time editing books and directing broadcasts for the purposes of propaganda aimed at audiences overseas. But she was not able to finish her work there. Philip Noel-Baker – the MP, Olympic medallist, Nobel prizewinner and Megan Lloyd George's lover for twenty years – ran into Matheson one day in June 1940 as he left the Ministry of Information, and remembered realising that she seemed terribly ill; he urged her to rest, but she told him that she needed to go on working, or 'everything may smash'. By this time her affair with Sackville-West was long over, and she had been living with Dorothy Wellesley, the poet. In October 1940 she was dead, at fifty-two, of Graves' disease – an autoimmune disorder affecting the thyroid. The Hogarth Press produced a short obituary volume, in which H. G. Wells paid tribute to a woman who was 'courageous and indefatigable in her work for that liberal thought and free expression which is the essence of democratic freedom. She maintained a steady fight against Sir John Reith, who was inspired by a loyalty to influences above him far stronger than any sense of duty to the greater possibilities of his position.' Composer Ethel Smyth wrote of the 'blending of her intellectual grip with what one may call the perfect manners of her soul'.

Matheson's name is largely lost now, but as a pioneering and visionary figure in the BBC over the short but formative period of 1926–31, she deserves a more generous place in history. Her insights into the nature of broadcasting – observations made when the wireless was newborn and with all its possibilities ready to unfold – still stand as fresh and optimistic and clear-sighted. She wrote to Sackville-West, '*The* thing broadcasting does, or can do, its chief claim to any virtue as far as the spoken word is concerned, is that it provides not a silent-printed word, a dead word if you like, but a living and very personal contact with an individual. The crucially affectionate link that grows between listeners and announcers, between listeners and regular broadcasters . . . is something quite peculiar to broadcasting.' She wrote in *Broadcasting* a sort of spec for a successful commissioning editor – the kind of manifesto that could still do good service for the BBC commissioners of today:

Broadcasters . . . must be sympathetic to new ideas, new personalities, new methods; they must indeed have a quite peculiar open-mindedness and a gift for personal contacts . . . Above all they must have an interest in human nature in its most varied shapes. Broadcasters can never rest; they are never off duty . . . they cannot escape the persistent questionmarks which face them everywhere – is there a new idea for me here? Have I overlooked this sort of man, woman or child in my programme building? What do these people think of broadcasting? Where does it fail them? What impresses them most? How could broadcasting handle this problem, reproduce that impression, convey those sounds? Would this sound be exciting? Would that be amusing?

She captured something of the anxiety attached to this new form of mass communication – something that resonates with the preoccupations of our own era, as history takes further technological leaps. She saw that some would be resistant – would be asking, 'How can we escape from this new noise that is adding to the distractions of an already complex world? Is it to be yet another byproduct of man's inventive mind which will get beyond his control before he has learnt its power?' But broadcasting, she argued – 'a harnessing of elemental forces, a capturing of sounds and voices all over the world to which hitherto we have been deaf' – was a wonderful, almost miraculous phenomenon, capable of magnificent things. 'It is a means of enlarging the frontiers of human interest and consciousness, of widening personal experience, of shrinking the earth's surface,' she wrote. 'Broadcasting as we know it, moreover, is in its infancy; it is comparable to the rudest scratchings on the cave-man's dark walls, to the guttural sounds which served the first homo sapiens for speech.' What a destiny Matheson foresaw. What a future to live up to.

3

Inform, Educate, Entertain

In the early years of the 1930s, the sculptor Eric Gill was commissioned to carve an image of a sower for the entrance hall of Broadcasting House. 'Broadcast' is the old word for scattering seed: you cast it far and wide and good things grow. As a preacher stands in the pulpit and hopes that the congregation will be improved by the word of God, so John Reith the minister's son cast the seeds of virtue into Britain. The BBC was to 'inform, educate and entertain': Reith carefully placed the words in that order. The Latin inscription in the hallway of Old Broadcasting House, through which workers still hurry to their offices at Radios 3 and 4, translates like this: 'This temple of the arts and muses is dedicated to Almighty God by the first Governors in the year of our Lord 1931, John Reith being director general. And they pray that good seed sown may bring forth good harvest, and that all things foul or hostile to peace may be banished thence, and that the people inclining their ear to whatsoever things are honest, whatsoever things are lovely, whatsoever things are of good report, may tread the path of virtue and wisdom.' The partial source of this ringing statement of intent was biblical: Philippians 4:8.

But what lovely things are to be scattered? From its earliest days the BBC was a culturally polyglot organisation, a clash of aesthetic tones. Hilda Matheson veered culturally towards modernism: she broadcast James Joyce reading from work-in-progress – not at all to the taste of Reith. 'It would be idle to pretend everybody liked them or understood [the readings],' she acknowledged in *Broadcasting*. 'Difficult, obscure, experimental literature . . . is unlikely to make a wide appeal.' Reith himself was conservative and traditionalist, as Harold Nicolson complained to his diary. They had been discussing the series of talks on modern literature he was to give, commissioned by Matheson. 'The man's head is made entirely of bone . . . [He] tries to induce me to modify my talks in such a way as to induce the illiterate members of the population to read Milton instead of going on bicycle excursions. I tell him that as my talk series centres upon literature of the last 10 years it would be a little difficult to say anything about Milton.'

Listeners had their own ideas, and many were impatient with BBC highmindedness – whether Reithian or Mathesonian in texture. In the first issue of the *Radio Times*, 28 September 1923, a reader's letter ran: 'Frankly, it seems to me that the BBC are mainly catering for the "listeners" who . . . pretend to appreciate only and understand only highbrow music and educational and "sob" stuff. Surely, like a theatre manager, they must put up programmes which will appeal to the majority and must remember that it is the latter who provide the main bulk of their income.' Similar debates persist today. Why does the BBC bother with niche culture, to be enjoyed only by a few, some ask. Others wonder why it promulgates mass culture, which, they argue, the market could easily provide. Arguably, though, it is precisely the dialectical tension between these two positions, the noisy jumble of cultures within the BBC, that has been one of its strongest and most exciting characteristics.

In 1935, the pioneering documentary-maker John Grierson made a film about the corporation for the GPO Film Unit (a department of the Post Office set up to make films mostly about its own activities). It was called *BBC: The Voice of Britain*. The two musical stars of the film were Adrian Boult, the conductor of the BBC Symphony Orchestra, and the toe-tappingly brilliant Henry Hall, band leader of the BBC Dance Orchestra. Between them they represented the extreme edges of rarefied and populist culture then projected by the BBC. There is a similar bifurcation in the way the film portrays drama: while the film shows the delightfully home-made sound effects being created for a broadcast of *Macbeth*, the lighter end is represented by head of variety Eric Maschwitz, seen urging a producer to make sure a music-hall act's jokes are cleaned up ('It won't get by for a moment, old boy').

Maschwitz had been one of the early BBC employees who had populated the young corporation's headquarters in Savoy Hill – 'at one time . . . a slightly risqué block of flats where I had attended my first theatrical party in 1917'. It was dingy but it was exciting, and it was full of talented, adventurous young people. Reith's personal discomfort with Maschwitz's brand of entertainment was evident: he would turn up to rehearsals 'at which he loomed over the awestruck performers like an anxious pike in a tank filled with tropical fish'. Maschwitz remembered how anarchic it was. Reith, 'his dour handsome face scarred like that of a villain in a melodrama', was 'a strange shepherd for such a mixed, bohemian flock . . . he had under his aegis a bevy of ex-soldiers, ex-actors, ex-adventurers which . . . even a Dartmoor prison governor might have had difficulty in controlling'.

Under Val Gielgud, brother of John, radio drama was developing as a form. It was 'finding wings; like the cinema before it, it was on its way to escaping from the limitations of theatre', recalled Maschwitz. Rather wonderfully, the makers of the earliest original radio drama, Richard Hughes's *A Comedy of Danger* (1924), were so anxious about the visual limitations of the medium that it was set in the pitch-blackness of a coal mine. (For similar reasons the earliest Italian operas tended to feature the character of Orpheus, as if to answer the question, 'Why are the characters singing?') Arthur Burrows, the BBC's first director of programmes, remembered, 'I think all who heard this first attempt at building up a really dramatic situation entirely by sound effects will admit that it was very thrilling, and opened up a wide range of possibilities.' BBC radio is now the biggest single commissioner of plays in the world, an artery in the great body of British dramatic writing.

The previous year, in January 1923, one of the earliest outside broadcasts of opera had taken place: *The Magic Flute*, performed from Covent Garden by the National Opera Company, one of the few musical or theatrical organisations that unhesitatingly decided to cooperate with the BBC from the start. Burrows's colleague Cecil

Lewis, a First World War fighter pilot and author of *Sagittarius Rising*, gave a vivid account of its impact. He and others had assembled in Marconi House, then the BBC headquarters, to listen: 'Our excitement was immense. The broadcasting of opera was an assured success – that could be said after listening for a few moments. The sound of the great orchestras contrasted so forcibly with our little band of seven in the studio that it came as a revelation of what the future of broadcasting might be . . .' As for the listeners: 'Many people imagining opera to be a dull and dreary thing were converted in an evening; many others who had never heard or expected to hear opera as long as they lived had it brought to their hospital or bedside.' In a time when we can hear any music with a mere click of a mouse, it is hard to imagine just how extraordinary this access to the sequestered sounds of Covent Garden must have been.

While Maschwitz presided over such acts as the Dancing Daughters – a troupe of teenage tap dancers, costumed skimpily in the studio 'to get the atmosphere' despite being invisible to the audience – another figure, whose name is now almost lost to public memory, was moulding the BBC's multifarious cultural mix. Edward Clark, who worked at the BBC between 1924 and 1936, was the son of a Newcastle coal exporter. Obsessed with music, and from a musical family, he persuaded his father to let him study abroad, as any Briton then seriously contemplating a musical career would do. In 1907 he set forth to Paris, then Vienna and Berlin, to learn the art of conducting. According to Dr Jenny Doctor, who has studied Clark and

his contribution to the BBC, as a musician he was 'talented
– but not supertalented. He was very good at seeing
opportunities, and saw that the way to make it was to get
to know the most significant people in music. He was very
starry-eyed when it came to the big names.' In Paris he
courted Debussy and Ravel, but the crucial meeting of his
life was with Arnold Schoenberg, whom he even helped
move from Vienna to Berlin when his career as a painter
and composer was failing. 'As he talked he looked through
you, incinerating your doubts or hesitations, making
equivocation impossible,' Clark recalled of the composer
in 1952. In his turn Schoenberg, in a diary entry of 1912,
noted of Clark, 'Remarkable; he knows no Wagner operas,
nothing by Mozart, nothing by Beethoven. But he wants
to be a conductor!! And he has often seen [Strauss's]
Elektra! . . . He blames it on musical conditions in
England.'

Clark was interned in Germany through the First
World War; afterwards, returning to Britain, he assisted
Adrian Boult as conductor of Diaghilev's Ballets Russes,
and then joined the BBC's regional service at Newcastle
as music director of its orchestra. He was noticed in
London (as perhaps one would be if one conducted the
orchestral world premiere of Schoenberg's *Verkläte Nacht*)
and, after the Newcastle station orchestra was disbanded,
he was brought down to Savoy Hill in 1927 as a programme planner. Once there, he became a crucial carrier
of the modern music of Continental Europe into British
homes, and an important force in changing those 'musical conditions in England'. Under his curatorship, music

by the great contemporary European composers was performed by the BBC: he had Anton Webern over to conduct his Five Movements for String Orchestra for broadcast; invited Igor Stravinsky to perform his own piano concerto on air, and Paul Hindemith his own viola concerto. In 1934 he broadcast a complete performance of Alban Berg's *Wozzeck*, no easy listen. According to Doctor, the reaction of the British public at hearing this kind of music was not quite what one might expect. To many listeners, it was not just modern music that was unfamiliar, but classical music altogether. 'Many people hadn't even heard a symphony orchestra in 1922 – and certainly not an opera,' said Doctor. 'Bach cantatas were just as unfamiliar as Schoenberg.' New music arrived on the wireless in an uproar of 'new' noise.

One of Clark's most lasting contributions was his devising of the idea of the BBC Symphony Orchestra – a group of committed, salaried players, in contrast to the norm, a shifting cast of freelance players, who could perform in flexible combinations and in a variety of musical styles. Along with the other four BBC orchestras, it is still an important mainstay of British cultural life, and has been the backbone of the BBC Proms since its formation. (The Proms, founded in 1895 by Sir Henry Wood, were taken over by the BBC in 1927 after they lost financial support from the music publisher Chappell.) The BBCSO was among the earliest orchestras to hold 'blind auditions'. As Matheson noted in *Broadcasting*, 'All auditions for the orchestra were made in such a way that the judges could hear but not see the players, which rendered a completely objective judgement more certain, and which, among other things, threw membership of the orchestra open equally to women and men.' Under Boult – its versatile if not always sublimely brilliant first music director – the orchestra's calling card was to be its performance of new music – 'novelties', in the parlance of the day. According to Doctor, 'Clark sold the BBC the idea that if you wanted to put the BBCSO on a par with the musical organisations of Continental Europe, if you wanted to establish a tradition, you must establish the tradition of the new.'

Clark married a singer, Dorothy, Dolly for short. After having a son, they separated, and while Dolly was working as a secretary at the BBC she met and later married the BBC's first chief engineer, Peter Eckersley. Clark's second wife was the composer Elisabeth Lutyens. She remembered the occasion on which they met – this was after his departure from the BBC – at the 'brandy stage' of a lunch with film director Basil Wright and composer Alan Rawsthorne at the Casa Prada Italian restaurant on the Euston Road, one of Clark's haunts. In strolled 'an elegant, "European-looking" gentleman in a white silk open-necked shirt and short blue linen coat . . . in his buttonhole the dark red clove carnation he invariably sported'.

He certainly cut a striking figure around town. In 1933 a writer for the *Sunday Express* wrote of him thus: 'Think of him as the perpetrator and prime promoter of all the Hindemith, Schoenberg and Stravinsky that you hear (or don't hear – I've often wondered) and you will want to throw a brick. Meet him, and you will immediately be charmed . . . Talks well, knows the best and cheapest restaurants and a good wine.' But he was not a man suited to institutional life. He infuriated his colleagues with administrative bungles and missed deadlines; his salary had to be paid in cash because he did not 'do' bank accounts. According to Lutyens's memoir, before they met he would think little of taking not one but two girlfriends on a European jaunt, expenses paid by the BBC. He also had a volcanic temper: early in their relationship, an unsuccessful struggle to open a bottle of Tio Pepe caused an outburst: a 'sudden, almost frightening and total rage ... I had never seen the like ... comparable to the vent of high explosive. It was so unexpected, so unnecessary and I was so unprepared – and somehow it was no laughing matter'.

The young BBC of the 1920s could accommodate such eccentricity and waywardness, just, though Clark's file in the BBC archives is peppered with complaints and anxieties. In 1926, while still at Newcastle, it was noted of him that 'a rather serious defect ... due to his temperament is that in times of stress his language is most unpleasant. This is the main reason why he has a man for his typist clerk.' That same year he wrote to a colleague of money, 'I have an absolute horror of the subject in any shape of form', and indeed his career was peppered by a series of financial scrapes from which the BBC wearily extracted him. (One employee in the administration department noted that 'Edward Clark is not quite normal from the financial and economic point of view'.) He was also highly disorganised and maddening to work with. One memo complained that he was 'one of those nervy neurotic people with whom it is very difficult to reason'. Cecil Graves, about to become assistant director of programmes (he rose to be a wartime DG) noted, 'While I realise that Clark is in himself a likeable person, he pulls absolutely no weight here and in fact hinders and hampers other people's work'. His skills as a conductor were also doubted by his boss in the music department, Kenneth Wright, in an internal memo: 'So far as his conducting is concerned, I think you saw that he did not make a marvellous job of the Stravinsky . . . Stravinsky was very irritated by the amount of time wasted by Clark at the rehearsals . . . the same applies to Bartók'. In January 1928, there was also a touch of panic about his role in rehearsals for Schoenberg's massive orchestral and choral work *Gurrelieder*, whose British premiere Clark had engineered. Despite his linguistic skills, he was 'useless as an interpreter' according to Wright and bungled the rehearsal schedule; when the women of the choir failed to turn up 'Schoenberg apparently blasphemed'. But it is thanks to Clark that the great flowerings of modernism from Europe – what Boult's predecessor Percy Pitt dismissively called 'certain foreign novelties' – were introduced to British homes for the first time. As the 1930s wore on, this disorganised, rule-breaking man could no longer fit in, and, after a series of rows, resigned on 16 March 1936. Lutyens summed up his contribution: 'Edward was first and foremost European-minded, with an equal interest in all the arts and creative phenomena of all the countries in Europe, not just the small parish of British music . . . He had a mind and outlook that expanded the narrow confines of music in England at that time.'

This expansion of the parochial horizons of British culture was also aided by a steady stream into the country, before the Second World War, of Jewish and anti-Nazi exiles, a number of whom joined the BBC. Among them was Martin Esslin (born Pereszlényi Gyula Márton in Budapest) who worked for the External Services and ran radio drama in the 1960s and 1970s, and Stephen Hearst (born Stephen Hirshtritt in Vienna) who was head of BBC TV arts features in the 1960s and ran Radio 3 in the 1970s. Another was the Frankfurt-born Ludwig Koch. As a child violinist he had been part of Clara Schumann's circle; his earliest memory was of being kissed by Liszt; and he had been advised to take singing lessons by Giuseppe Verdi. In adulthood Koch became an important sound recordist of the natural world, in his time as familiar a name to BBC audiences as David Attenborough is today.

In Penelope Fitzgerald's wartime BBC novel *Human Voices* Koch is given fictional life as Dr Vogel, an émigré who, in pursuit of a programme called *Lest We Forget Our Englishry*, travels round the country recording people's wheezy breathing and endless creaking church doors. The name Vogel is a pun on the title of Koch's autobiography, *Memoirs of a Birdman*, *Vogel* being the German for 'bird'. At the start of that book, Koch describes being given an Edison phonograph and a box of wax cylinders by his father in 1889, when he was eight. 'I had the original idea of using my phonograph to record human voices,' he remembered, in a pre-echo of the title of Fitzgerald's novel.

As a child he collected 'audio autographs' – Kaiser Wilhelm's curiously high-pitched voice among them – as well as 'the voices of all the Bayreuth Wagner singers of the late-90s' and birdsong, including 'the raucous call of the great bustard'. All these early recordings were lost during the war. 'All gone with the Nazis. Well, it can't be helped,' he once told an interviewer. When coaching singers at Bayreuth he discussed *The Ride of the Valkyries* with Cosima Wagner: her husband had been inspired by the throbbing, panting sound of the mute swan's wingbeat, she told him. With his wife Nellie in Frankfurt, Koch kept a bewildering menagerie at home of 68 creatures. Nellie remembered the surprising morning when 'there were suddenly two alligators on the breakfast table in cardboard boxes!'

Koch pioneered an early version of the multimedia text: what he called the 'soundbook', which combined recorded sounds with a written commentary, an especially useful tool in the field of ornithology. But working in Germany became increasingly dicey in the 1930s, and during a trip to Switzerland, where he had been seen talking to a Nazi official who was shortly afterwards assassinated, he was warned not to return. 'I landed at Dover on 17 February 1936, and arrived in London alone and almost penniless, at 5 p.m., welcomed by mist and drizzling rain,' he recalled in his autobiography. (Cold and damp was to be a recurring theme: 'As I write this I have been here 18 years and yet I still cannot understand the average British person's love of draughts and cold rooms.')

Only a week after arriving in London Koch received a letter from Mary Adams, of the BBC's talks department, and gradually began to be offered work. After a period of internment on the Isle of Man (where 'I was able to make a special study of the hooded crow and the herring gull'), he joined the staff of the BBC, his task to build up the sound-effects library. 'I visited a number of factories to explore unusual noises, but amid the din of machinery I longed for the sounds of nature, and I persuaded my superiors that this was the right moment to show the enemy, by recording all kinds of farm animals, that even bombing could not entirely shatter the natural peace of this island,' he remembered. He composed a 'Victory Symphony' from found sounds mimicking the opening of Beethoven Five – 'even nature helped me, for one of the call-notes of the curlew has this victory rhythm'. Internal BBC documents detail his recordings: one memo concerning 'Dr Ludwig Koch, 19 October 1942', is headed, delightfully, 'An exhaustive series of recordings of footsteps, probably out of doors'. Another note, written on the same day, contains a list of his recordings that reads like a taxonomy out of a Borges story: bugle calls, aircraft factory, farm animals, winnowing, St Paul's Cathedral in wartime, pigs and sow, donkey braying, concolor gibbons, black-necked crackle, yellowhammer, demolition and reconstruction, tank factory, steam and hand winch, derrick and rope running out, conversation on quay re cargo, footsteps on pavement.

By January 1943 the head of the BBC's sound library, Marie Slocombe, was despairing of Koch, whose high professional standards often prompted him to spend a great deal more time and money on projects than his employer deemed necessary. Though his work was 'excellent beyond dispute' he was 'constantly straining at the leash and going beyond his terms of reference, and quite frankly wastes a lot of my time in attempts to discuss the most far-reaching schemes which are quite irrelevant and quite impracticable'. He certainly inspired BBC employees to unaccustomed heights of burnished prose. 'To explain to him that Effects records could be continued without him is rather like trying to explain to Kreisler that it is possible for other people to play *Caprice Viennoise*. This does not mean Dr Koch is conceited. He just cannot understand how anyone can regard perfection as a luxury', noted the recorded programmes director in January 1943.

Fitzgerald cruelly killed off her Dr Vogel in *Human Voices* – she downed him with a piece of flying drainpipe in the Blitz, as he courteously attempted to explain a point of English law to an ARP warden. The real Koch returned to freelance life, constantly attempting to persuade the BBC of the immense care and time required to maintain his desired standards. This was particularly true of his recordings of birds: even to get sufficiently close to his often rare or shy targets, with the bulky equipment of the 1940s, could be an extraordinary feat, requiring a naturalist's knowledge, the cunning of a thief and the patience of a saint. A typical letter, from 24 August 1946, written somehow in a strong German accent, runs:

Last spring I have been concentrating under horrid conditions watching by day and night the breeding behaviour of the Green-shank and made an attempt to record as many breeding notes as possible, especially the cracking of the eggshells and the first peeping of the youngsters and the mother talking to the young birds is very fascinating. But with these recordings the bird is not covered yet and I intend to spend at least one or even two more months somewhere in the Highlands, early next spring, trying to get the courtship notes of the bird, including the wonderful song.

Koch also contributed a series of programmes to the BBC after the war called 'sound pictures'. One especially delicious example was a compilation, without voiceover or interruption, of noises harvested from a beach. He introduced it thus:

Throughout the ages, the eye of mankind has always been kept in training . . . but sound has never been preserved for us. I notice that very few people really listen, either to the radio or natural sounds, or even to beautiful mechanical sounds out of doors such as church bells or carillons. Most people still use their radio as a daily background to work or conversation. I want you to concentrate only for quarter of an hour. Close your eyes. Do not fall to sleep. Simply listen . . .

There follows the susurration of waves lapping at the sand; the cry of melancholy seabirds, the buzz of a motor-launch engine and the voices of distant, happy children. 'War or no war, bird life is going on and even the armed power of the three dictators cannot prevent it,' he had written a few years earlier in a letter to *The Times*. 'I would like to advise everybody in a position to do so, to relax his nerves, in listening to the songs, now so beautiful, of the British birds.' In his voice, the injunction becomes almost an act of resistance. To stop, to open your ears, to delight in bird-song: to grip humanity close though war raged.

Huw Wheldon – D-day war hero and founder, in 1958, of the first TV arts programme *Monitor*, nursery of Ken Russell, John Schlesinger, Humphrey Burton and Melvyn Bragg – invented a ringing phrase to describe the BBC's cultural mission. It was about making 'the good popular and the popular good'. But doing so has never been as simple or as uncontested as his neatly balanced chiasmus implies. Within the BBC, the politics of 'inform, educate and entertain' have been fought over, the Reithian inheritance ferociously debated and subjected to widely differing interpretations. In the BBC that Wheldon worked in, music programmer William Glock was taking forward Clark's inheritance and introducing listeners of the Third Programme to a new generation of the European avant-garde. Now audiences could hear music by composers such as Pierre Boulez, who would become the BBC Symphony Orchestra's chief conductor from 1971 to 1975. Glock took the view, he remembered in his memoir *Notes in Advance* (1991), that 'to try to give the public "what it wants" inevitably means falling below its potential standards and appetites'.

Over in television, Bill Cotton, the man who would become the head of light entertainment at the BBC in 1970, and later managing director of television in the 1980s, had a different view on the relative importance of the tricolon 'inform, educate and entertain'. He and

Wheldon, he remembered in his autobiography, 'both believed that the BBC's core duty was to entertain the public, for the simple reason that unless listeners and viewers found a programme agreeable they wouldn't stay with it long enough to be educated or informed'.

Cotton, the son of the wildly popular band leader Billy Cotton, himself a fixture on post-war BBC television, described himself in his memoir *Double Bill* (2000) as representing the 'vulgar end of the market'. In an age of ratings battles with ITV, he invented *Top of the Pops*, and had the idea of a show for Jimmy Savile called *Jim'll Fix It*. ('Jim', he recalled, in what now seems ominous phrasing, 'could get kids to do anything.') He brought Morecambe and Wise into the BBC, had the idea of asking Ronnie Corbett and Ronnie Barker to form a double act, and, borrowing the format from a Dutch show he encountered at a European awards ceremony, devised the hugely popular *Generation Game*, which ran from 1971 to 1982 and was revived in the 1990s.

Cotton, steeped in show business, came from a different world from that of most of the decorously educated, solidly middle-class executives at the BBC. So did his protégé, Michael Grade, now Lord Grade. He was also the scion of an entertainment dynasty. His father, Leslie, and uncles, Bernie and Lew, were impresarios, agents and theatre owners. Michael Grade ran BBC1 in the 1980s and eventually became the BBC's chairman (2004–6). Lew, Leslie and Bernie were born the Winogradskys, sons of a family that had emigrated from Ukraine in 1905 to two rooms over a shoe shop in the East End of London. Lew started out dancing the charleston in East Ham, becoming an agent for music-hall and variety acts when his knees started to give out when he was twenty-seven; he rose to become a mogul of commercial television. The Grade family story – a remarkable ascent from Brick Lane to presiding over the BBC within two generations – is in itself a metaphor of the manner in which popular British entertainment shifted from the stage to the small screen, and a reminder of how powerful the impresarios of popular entertainment were within the BBC, especially one that was competing with ITV for eyes on screen.

When the writer Dennis Potter was asked about television for *The New Priesthood* (1970), a volume on television co-edited by Joan Bakewell, he told her, 'The main criticism with television is that it just seems an endlessly grinding thing – a burning monk, an advertisement, and Harold Wilson, and a pop show, and Jimmy Savile, all seem the same sort of experience.' But, on the other hand, compared with the 'middle-class privilege of the theatre, only television is classless, multiple, and, of course, people will switch on and people will choose. It's the biggest platform in the world's history, and writers who don't want to kick and elbow their way onto it must be disowning something in themselves.' The BBC, he said, 'does genuinely give one the chance to create . . . I think it's a federation, really, of various pressure groups. The *Wednesday Play* as a unit became, as it were, its own little force within this huge stadium called the BBC.'

In the 1960s, the *Wednesday Play* put out Ken Loach films such as *Cathy Come Home* and Potter's own *Vote,*

Vote, Vote for Nigel Barton. It was a purple patch in the BBC's cultural history: a time when the right people and conditions for making great art collided. Stephen Frears, now best known for feature films, directed in the BBC in the 1970s, often working on Alan Bennett's TV plays, starting with *A Day Out* (1972). He was operating in Loach's slipstream. Loach had, he said, 'just invented television films. I mean he literally invented them.'

Absorbing the influence of the Italian neo-realists and Czech cinema, 'he had stumbled on a whole new story of Britain which had never really been told', added Frears. 'The BBC had a great subject: working-class, post-war Britain was being revealed.' Frears, a bearlike, crumpled man whom I met at his regular cafe in Notting Hill, said, 'I tell you what: it's really the growth of management you should be writing about. One man ran the drama department. You fitted into a process that was a perfectly intelligent process, and you were working with the best writers, it seemed to me, in the country. I could see if you weren't one of the writers they were interested in you wouldn't agree with me but – Tom Stoppard, Alan Bennett, Adrian Mitchell. What are you supposed to do? Complain?' Bright people were lurking down every corridor 'and it sort of rubbed off on you. It was a very creative time.'

It is dangerous to look back to the BBC's past and identify golden ages (and a flick through back issues of the *Radio Times* puts paid to such notions: there has always been plenty of forgettable or mediocre programming among the wonderful stuff). In truth, there have been moments when artists and the times aligned and great things were created: one thinks of *Monty Python* and its successors, or the emergence of the alternative comedians of the 1980s such as French and Saunders, Rory Bremner and Victoria Wood, figures whom the then head of light entertainment, Jim Moir, deliberately sought out to give comedy on BBC2 a different flavour from that of its sister channel.

Ask those involved in these moments of creative blooming, and they will often tell you much the same thing: 'management' was discreet and enabling; artists were free to experiment; commissioning was not mired in lengthy bureaucracy; the stakes were relatively low and ambition high; failure was an option. Some argue that those conditions are in much shorter supply now. The often-expressed tension between 'creatives' and 'managers' has always been there. Matheson wrote, 'There is a constant pull between the claims of administration and creation. Under what conditions shall the creative worker serve? Ideally he needs quiet, freedom from routine, time in which to lie fallow after a big piece of work, time to go to and fro seeking inspiration. Such behaviour may seem another name for idling to the rigid administrator.'

Sir David Attenborough's career has spanned both creative work and administration. He was the second controller of BBC2 – which launched in 1964 – from 1965 to 1969. At the beginning, only a handful of people had the new sets capable of receiving the service, and at first it was available only in the south-east. We talked in his new library, built onto the house in Richmond where he has lived since the 1950s: a galleried, top-lit space with a grand piano in its centre (Haydn sonatas on the stand) and set about with African sculptures and his collection of modern British studio ceramics. The walls were lined with thousands of art books, all neatly arranged by type from Aegean art to Indian sculpture. The natural history library, presumably yet more vast, was elsewhere.

The principle behind BBC2 was that it should not be higher brow than the BBC, but distinct from it. 'The idea that you could do it by height of brow was nonsense. I mean there are plenty of people who like string quartets and plenty of people who like football, and plenty of people who like both, and so just to put on chamber music opposite football was irrelevant,' he said. At the same time, 'it felt very free, creatively free, because you couldn't use the normal statistics, because the audience was changing all the time, because the coverage [of the transmitters] was changing all the time. I mean it was a doddle of a job. I was shielded from the pressures that BBC1 was taking.' He added, 'Occasionally I get nice compliments for inventing *Civilisation* [Sir Kenneth Clark's series on Western art]. They say, "How brave." It wasn't in the least brave. It was just that I thought it was a good idea. And there was nobody with a big stick saying, "Naughty, naughty, you didn't get 3 million viewers, you only got 2.5 [million]." And that was why it was the dream job, running BBC2. A paradisiacal job.'

Civilisation had endured as a classic series, he argued, because of its great writing, and the power of Clark as an intellect and a communicator. Attenborough despaired of some of its successors. He picked out as typical a

The young David Attenborough, behind the camera

programme that had been aired just before we met: *Apples, Pears and Paint: How to Make a Still Life Painting*. 'It had a typical crappy kind of sense of "Oh we can't have a mandarin point of view, so what you will do is to get 10 different people, we'll interview them and then we'll just sling little slices of it together." And so there's no thesis, there's no continuity, there's no central thought . . . it was exasperating, empty-headed. The trouble is that we live in a populist culture where we can't accept that there's anybody who actually knows more about things than you do.' Broadcasting, he said, 'should be the cream of thinkers in society who have been given by the BBC a platform on which they may speak. But the BBC doesn't believe that now.'

An early programme on BBC2, commissioned by Atten-borough's predecessor, Michael Peacock, was *The Great War*. Marking fifty years since the war began, it mixed archive footage with testimony from survivors, and was the first of the great blockbuster history series on television – the progenitor of Jeremy Isaacs's classic series for Thames, *The World at War*. The idea for it came from producers Antony Jay and Alasdair Milne, the buccaneering young-sters who had been making a splash with *Tonight*, the early-evening current affairs show. At first the notion was simply to find a way of showing archive footage held by the Imperial War Museum. But the young guns decided to treat *The Great War* as if they were putting together *Tonight* – 'approaching the world today with a popular voice', in the words of historian and producer Taylor Downing.

And so the importance of *The Great War* was that it gave voice to the everyday veterans of the conflict. An advert in the *Radio Times*, asking for contributors, resulted in about 30,000 responses. The researcher, Julia Cave, 're-turned from her holiday barely able to get in through the door of her office', said Downing. General Montgomery (in the First World War a junior officer) wrote to the *Daily Telegraph* offering to be interviewed, but the producers were not interested in the man who later commanded the Eighth Army. This was not to be a parade of famous names. Despite its shortcomings (it had little time for women and the manner in which it failed to distinguish archive footage from feature film sequences would be deemed unacceptable today), it was intensely true to the possibilities of television as a form. It gave voice to

That's Life! mixed campaigning journalism with lighter items.
(From left) Michael Groth, Bill Buckly, Esther Rantzen, Gavin
Campbell (top), Doc Cox (bottom), Joanna Monro.

ordinary people, captured evanescent human experience.
It was ahead of academia, which had yet to embrace oral
history. It showed that television could act as a nation's
generous and reflective memory bank, drawing in the
breath of lived lives and projecting them back into ordinary homes. Its title sequence might have come from a
Bergman film: a cross is bleakly silhouetted against a grey
sky; then the camera pans down to the base of a trench,
where a corpse lies, horribly contorted. This against an

intense score by Wilfred Josephs. The ambition was both epic and deeply humane.

At its best, the important thing about the BBC has always been its cultural heterogeneity; the fact that it is a cheerful gallimaufry of the high and the low, the serious and the silly. Television has been the perfect medium for reflecting what BBC documentary-maker Adam Curtis called, when we met at New Broadcasting House, 'the libertarian revolution that's happened in this country: the breaking down of cultural barriers, the breaking down of social barriers. The mixture that the BBC invented – trash shows, and posh, clever, high-end shows – has been appropriate to its time.'

As a young man, he was a researcher on the popular consumer programme *That's Life!* under Esther Rantzen, which mixed campaigning investigative journalism with joke items on talking dogs and curiously shaped vegetables. Now he is known for highly wrought political documentaries, such as *Pandora's Box* (1992) and *The Power of Nightmares* (2004) – which he said he made cheaply by 'swimming between the cracks': improvising, borrowing and making do within the 'chaotic' structures of the BBC. But he uses what he learned from Rantzen: she taught him, he said somewhat self-deprecatingly, the 'tricks of trash journalism. I took them and bolted them on to high-end meta-tosh.'

His fellow researcher was the youthful Peter Bazalgette, who ended up as chair of the UK arm of Endemol Productions, and who made 1990s lifestyle shows such as *Changing Rooms* and *Ground Force*. He also used Rantzen's tricks.

'There is an alchemy', said Bazalgette, 'whereby you take factual information, which has some connection, umbilical or tangential, to public service, and you make it entertaining. How do you make it entertaining? You inject humanity and narrative. That's what I learned from her.' His shows were like old-fashioned instructional DIY or cookery shows – but with fun and story attached, just as *That's Life!* mingled humour with reporting on serious issues.

The television later made by Bazalgette and Curtis could hardly, on the surface, be more different, and yet their work, each in its own way, is the product of a superlatively televisual miscegenation. The point, Melvyn Bragg told me, is that the BBC has historically recognised the voracious and various appetites within each of us. 'Everyone watched *Morecambe and Wise*, and *The Billy Cotton Band Show*. And because it was on television you could, as it were, watch it in secret.' By everyone, he meant intellectuals and highbrows, too. 'There it was, an insignificant object in the corner of a room; you could switch it on like an electric light, enjoy *Morecambe and Wise* without your friends knowing. Or, on the other hand, you could enjoy watching Elgar without your friends knowing.' This is the BBC: the avant-garde and the crowd-pleasing, the brash and the brilliant and the beautiful all together, many streams flowing into the same wide ocean.

In the end, it goes back to the sculpture of the sower. We could all tell our own stories about the moment we heard or saw something on the BBC that changed us: whether you were the oddball suburban kid who saw Ziggy Stardust on *Top of the Pops* and knew you weren't alone in the world; or whether you were like me, seeing Wagner's *Ring* on TV as a child and drawn into a mysterious, seductive world of gods and magic and warrior women.

Sir Richard Eyre, the former artistic director of the National Theatre, sometime BBC TV director and ex-BBC governor, remembers how important television was to him, growing up in Dorset in the 1950s. We met while he was rehearsing *The Pajama Game* in a church hall in Kensington in the summer of 2014. As I walked through the room to greet him, swarms of leotarded actors surged past, taking a break from the song-and-dance number they'd just hoofed through. 'We didn't have art galleries, didn't go to the theatre, didn't go to the cinema,' he told me. 'The books in the house were mostly military history. So the BBC was my education. *As You Like It* with Vanessa Redgrave was completely transformative; so was *Monitor* with Huw Wheldon . . . This was art that I hadn't dreamed existed. It was absolutely contagious and it changed my life. And it wouldn't have happened without the existence of the BBC.'

Dennis Potter had a similar story to tell when he addressed the Edinburgh Television Festival in 1993. The wireless of his childhood was like a totem or fetish: 'a whorled, fluted and beknobbed oblong which could allow anyone to feel like Joan of Arc'. He went on: 'I would not dispute for one wayward whistle or crackle that the BBC of my childhood was not paternalistic and often stuffily pompous. It saw itself in an almost priestly role. But at a crucial period of my life it threw open the "magic casement" on great sources of mind-scape at a time when books were hard to come by, and when I had never stepped into a theatre or even a concert hall, and would have been scared to do so even if given the chance.'

Matheson recalled that 'during the exceptionally severe frosts of 1929' she asked one of her talkers to read from Virginia Woolf's *Orlando* – 'the romantic chapter describing the great frost in Elizabethan London'. Some months later, the talker was being chauffeured by a 'young mechanic' in 'a large manufacturing town'. The mechanic said, 'I listened to your reading from a book about the frozen Thames. When you finished I was so excited I went out into the night and walked and walked, I don't know where. I would give anything to have that book.' The seed was sown.

4

'Television is a bomb about to burst': Grace Wyndham Goldie

On the night of 23 February 1950 the evening's television schedule began with the usual announcement of the programme. There would be films, including an American slapstick with Charley Chase; and, as customary, the 9 p.m. news delivered in sound only. But this was an exceptional evening: the night of the general election, with Clement Attlee's huge 1945 majority contested by Winston Churchill. The turnout that day was an immense 83.9 per cent. 'We shall be giving results', intoned the announcer, 'as they come in from 10.45 to round about one o'clock in the morning. They will be shown on charts, diagrams and maps with commentaries by R. B. McCallum of Pembroke College, Oxford, and David Butler of Nuffield – who made a special study of the 1945 election. And Chester Wilmot. We shall also go over to Trafalgar Square, where results will be flashed up on a large screen and where there will be commentary by Richard Dimbleby . . . And now, to open the programme, we have a film showing the latest types of British aircraft which were on show at Farnborough in September . . .'

Both television studios at Alexandra Palace were ready to go after a flurry of preparations and a blizzard of paperwork: in one there were 12-foot-tall maps on the walls, as well as a library ladder on wheels, a pointer, and sticks of charcoal; in the other, there was a chart laid out like a cricket scoreboard, another resembling a thermometer, and a board showing a 'list of personalities IN and OUT, according to the swiftly shuttling memos. The programme was due to continue well past the normal 10.30 p.m. close-down, despite dark prophecies from the engineering staff that 'you'll blow up the transmitters'. In the event, the engineer in charge settled for warning his team that though there would be late catering facilities, 'staff may find it an advantage if they produce a Thermos flask'.

Sitting in a row at oak desks were the anchorman, Australian former war reporter Wilmot, and the two election experts: McCallum, the political historian who coined the term 'psephology' (the study of votes cast); and his young protégé David Butler, then an Oxford postgraduate in his twenties, who was later one of the co-inventors of the 'swingometer' and who provided TV commentaries on the next nine elections, until 1979. Neither had appeared on the small screen before. In 2014, Butler, then ninety, remembered that 'by the end of that two days of the election, I'd spent more time in front of the cameras than I'd ever spent in front of the screen'. McCallum had told the producer that he 'knew nothing about television'. He began his spiel by explaining that 'this is more or less a normal election' – which was in itself, after the exceptional circumstances of the war, a novelty. 'The parliament just dissolved has lasted nearly its full legal time of five years. In 1945, we had a parliament ten years old, prolonged by statute throughout the war. It was the longest parliament which had sat in this country since the reign of Charles II

... Now we have had years of the regular cut-and-thrust of government and opposition. The public is ready for the election, and had been ready for months past.'

The election programme went on until shutdown at 2.13 a.m., shifting between Wilmot and the experts in the studio and Dimbleby in Trafalgar Square, where there was a live results board erected courtesy of the *Daily Mail* (confusingly, it was slightly out of sync with the results coming into Alexandra Palace). There had been endless kerfuffles about how most accurately to get the checked and verified results to the television studios – in the end they were telephoned in from Broadcasting House, where they were being collated for the wireless operation. Studio hands in gym shoes ran the results between Studios A and B. They were then handwritten on caption cards by volunteers from the design department. 'It took about forty seconds from the result being handed to the caption artist for them to put in the figures, and that was time enough for my people to use their slide rules, and then pass me a slip of paper with the result percentaged, so I could say, "A swing of such-and-such", remembered Butler when we met in the marbled foyer of the British Academy. His 'people' were fellow Oxford students, hidden just off camera to his right. Behind him, artists annotated the giant map of Britain by hand – white squares for Conservative vote, black for Labour and a grey-and-white stripe for Liberal.

The stakes were high: the BBC's future was under consideration by the Beveridge Parliamentary Committee and any hint of bias would have been a disaster. A memo from

Norman Collins, head of the television service, had made it clear before the night that 'though we are fully at liberty to analyse the results as they come through and draw such historic comparisons as may be relevant, we must scrupulously avoid anything that may be interpreted as political prophecy'. There would be no broadcasts of polling booths or counts: 'too politically invidious'. But the night went smoothly: there were no big gaffes. Butler in particular 'threw himself into the enterprise', remembered the programme's producer. 'He had a prodigious memory for detail, a taste for statistics, a total lack of nervousness of television cameras and an immense constructive and practical interest in methods of presentation.' Butler remembered the night as 'an adventure'. He added, 'I was doing what I'd been doing in private in public and I was quite quick with responses.' The political situation itself was less clear-cut: Attlee was returned to power with a majority of only six seats, and called an election the following year, when Churchill and the Conservatives were elected.

This programme established, from a standing start, the basic recipe for election-results programmes that is still followed today – an anchor and experts in the studio providing analysis aided by now unrecognisably whizzy graphics, along with outside broadcasts. And it was very largely the work of one woman: its producer, Grace Wyndham Goldie.

The programme was created, she remembered, in the teeth of an institutional indifference verging on hostility – what Butler called 'the obscurantist bits of Reithism that were surviving in the Beeb at that time'. Wireless still

Top Election night 1950: from left: David Butler,
R. B. McCallum, and Chester Wilmot
Above Grace Wyndham Goldie, pioneer of TV current affairs

reigned supreme at Broadcasting House. Television was something of an upstart: it 'could be brushed aside; it was not a medium to be taken seriously', as Goldie put it in her book *Facing the Nation*. There were innumerable technical and practical objections to her plans. She was supported by Collins (who, in a memo, enthusiastically envisaged 'some piece of apparatus like the score-board at Lord's' in the studio). But Tahu Hole, the head of news, was un-cooperative and Cecil McGivern, the head of television programmes, was discouraging, arguing that the way to tackle the results was simply to interrupt the evening's pro-gramme with the occasional shot of the board in Trafalgar Square. Goldie, however, immediately realised that the election was an event made for television – that there were possibilities of a quite different order from those offered by sound, which 'simply put on the results which came out from Reuters and the Press Association' with the gaps between announcements filled by light music.

The day Attlee called the election, she had been lunch-ing with Wilmot. 'There and then we cooked up . . . a plan, drawing pictures on the tablecloth,' she recalled in the 1970s. Statistics, share of vote, location of constituencies, the then emergent concept of 'swing': all of these were in-finitely easier to see than to take in by ear. Added to that, the election itself was a national drama; not merely a clash between Attlee and Churchill, not just a battle between 'two kings . . . fighting in the sunset' but an event contain-ing 'the dramatic quality of the actual. When you have events that are actually occurring and if you can see and hear them . . . it's the kind of drama that you get from nothing else,' she remembered. As she wrote later, the 1950 programme was a watershed moment: 'Producers were learning how to handle political occasions in ways which suited television without departing from the duty of the BBC to be fair, impartial and to refrain from expressing its own opinions.' There would, she predicted, be a profoundly equalising impact on British society: 'No one, not even a Macmillan or an Attlee, a Gaitskell or an Alec Douglas-Home, a Wilson, a Heath or a Margaret Thatcher, whose whole future and that of their parties depended upon the result, knew what it would be earlier than a shepherd in the Highlands or a housewife in Islington. The privilege of the few had once again been extended to the many.'

Grace Wyndham Goldie, remembered her protégé Alasdair Milne, was 'a small, birdlike woman with a striking finely chiselled face . . . a sharp questing mind and great charm'. Her physical delicacy was, to her colleagues, somewhat at odds with her character: she was articulate, persuasive, tough-minded and often intimidating: 'more eagle than wren', remembered David Attenborough, no mean ornithologist, in his autobiography. (When we met, he used another metaphor – a 'ferocious battleaxe'.) Butler remembered her as sometimes 'difficult and capricious'. It was said of her, he told me, that she was 'a woman of iron whim'. At the time of the election results programme she was forty-nine years old and had been working in television for a little less than three years. A photograph from the early 1950s shows her sitting in a studio gallery with banks of screens behind her, a clipboard on her lap, right hand brandishing a pen. Her hair is swept up neatly, there are pearls in her ears and a brooch at her breast. She radiates a certain practical glamour: but above all the air of a seasoned, competent professional woman.

Born Grace Nisbet in 1900, she was the child of a Scottish engineer who worked on the Mallaig railway and the Aswan Dam; much of her childhood was spent in Egypt. After a year at Cheltenham Ladies' College, at the tail end of the First World War, she enrolled at the University of Bristol and completed a history degree; afterwards she went up to study philosophy, politics and economics at Somerville College, Oxford. She tended to divide the world into those whom she regarded as in her intellectual league, and those with a 'dishevelled' brain. She taught history in a girls' school for a few years, and then married actor Frank Wyndham Goldie – with whom she had a deeply loving relationship until his early death in 1957. Butler remembered him as 'a very decent, wholesome man who greatly admired Grace'. They at first lived in Liverpool, where he was a member of the company at the Playhouse and she worked reading scripts and, in the evenings, lecturing for the Workers' Educational Association to 'unemployed miners' in the villages of Lancashire. In the 1970s she remembered the expectations that she and her highly educated female friends brought to their married life: 'If we'd got married any career that mattered was our husband's career and I had no intention of going on in any full-time job of any kind.'

In 1934, when Frank landed a substantial part at the Criterion Theatre, they moved to London. At a dinner party one night she turned to one of her fellow guests and 'we argued fairly hotly . . . about some political goings-on in Europe about which I have no doubt I was totally ignorant but had strong views nevertheless. And after this dinner party . . . I had a letter asking me to lunch and it was from this man with whom I'd argued at dinner.' The man turned out to be Richard Lambert, erstwhile colleague and admirer of Hilda Matheson (who had resigned three years previously). Lambert offered her the role of radio-drama critic on the BBC's magazine the *Listener*. Discussing the nature of the job over lunch with him and Val Gielgud, the BBC's head of plays, she asked what kind of criticism they had in mind. Gielgud pulled out of his pocket something written for one of the Manchester papers by D. G. Bridson, who had gone on to become a BBC producer. 'It was vitriolic, it was absolutely destructive beyond belief,' she remembered. 'And Val to my extreme astonishment said, "Now that's the sort of criticism I'd like."'

For the following seven years she contributed articles of crystalline clarity and occasional ferocity to the magazine. Her reviews show a particular sensitivity to the suitability of material to form; to the specific nature of radio, and to its capabilities and responsibilities. She admired Gielgud's understanding that audio was capable of creating magical worlds with no analogue in the 'real': 'a mysterious unreality in which he could make you participate', as she put it. She was merciless when the BBC failed to live up to her standards. Shortly after the outbreak of war, in her column for 28 September 1939, she railed against the drama department's production of a 'hackneyed, trivial and second-rate piece' – *Dr Abernethy*, a one-act play by Alicia Ramsey and Rudolph de Cordova that, according to Goldie, had been 'a standby of repertory theatre and amateur dramatic societies since the dark ages'. She concluded her review, 'It is to the BBC that we look for nourishment of the mind and spirit. Are we to look in vain? The times call for a bigness of idea and a sweep of the imagination beyond the ordinary . . . Well?'

In 1936 she had got wind of the BBC's experiments in television, the idea of which she found 'fascinating and extreme'. She asked Lambert if she could cover them for the journal. She remembered his response: 'Oh no, no, you don't want to go and see television . . . look television is going to be of no importance in your lifetime or mine and I don't want you to go up there wasting your time on it and you are certainly not going to write about it.' Let me go just to have a look out of curiosity, she pleaded. Off she traipsed to Alexandra Palace, where she watched – comparing the live action to the broadcast version on a monitor – a revue called *Here's Looking at You* (an obvious reference to the novelty of the medium) by variety producer Cecil Madden.

The production, she recalled, 'was terrible, the whole thing was terrible, the reception was awful and I was convinced this was going to become one of the most influential things that had ever been created'. She called Lambert from a phone box in Wood Green and demanded to be allowed to write about it. She was electrified; her wonderment (and perspicacity) shining through the article. 'I admit that the whole of this television business goes slightly to my head. I cannot get used to being a "viewer", she wrote. 'I find it difficult to realise this miracle, this phenomenon, is actually here and part of our daily lives. But it is . . . it was perfectly clear from the programmes I saw that television has arrived, not as a freak and a curiosity, but as successful everyday entertainment.' With characteristic clarity, she identified the essential qualities of the medium. It had 'a vividness which we cannot get from sightless broadcasting and a combination of reality and intimacy which we cannot get from the films', she wrote. Eventually she was to write weekly about television, grappling with the problems and possibilities of the nascent medium.

In 1948, she was to expand such thinking into a chapter of a book, *Made for Millions*, about the new era of mass communication. Television was, she said, 'a bomb about to burst' (rather a bold metaphor to employ so shortly after real bombs had ceased to fall). 'What is taking place, there, in front of us, on the lighted glass panel of our receiving sets, is not a photograph or a film. It is the real thing: a black-and-white, two-dimensional representation of reality produced electrically by the reflection of light from the real objects and the real people.' She was writing, of course, when studio television was essentially a live experience. History, in a way, has looped back to join her, since in the age of fractured viewing it is television-as-event, television-in-the-moment (such as, say, the 2012 Olympics) that has a special power to bring a dispersed audience back round a television to enjoy the same event simultaneously. She added, 'The "teleview" has what the newsreel has not – the dramatic quality of suspense. When we see a newsreel of the Derby, we know already what horse has won: but when we watch a teleview we do not know this, and, what is more, we know that no one knows it. A real event in television becomes, therefore, a shared experience; the people in the picture and the viewers watching them are bound together.' She considered, too, the particular quality of ordinariness that television has: the rise of reality shows in the 1990s would not, one suspects, have surprised her. 'The texture as well as the tempo of life is retained in television as it cannot be in the cinema,' she wrote. 'A thousand subjects of everyday routine which are too ordinary for the cinema become excellent television material.'

After war broke out Frank, though in his forties, volunteered – becoming one of the generation of men who served in both the First and Second World Wars. Money was short and Grace, with no children to care for, took a civil-service job, organising the distribution of essential household goods to parts of the country suffering shortages. It was valuable work in which she took enormous pride: devising systems to get pots and pans to bombed-out mothers stretched intellectual muscles that she had never used as a writer and critic. There was a rigour to the civil-service discourse, she found: 'If at a meeting you said something where you couldn't validate your suggestions by produced facts . . . you very quickly learned by the withering scorn round the table never to open your mouth in these circumstances again.'

Then, in 1944, a letter came from George Barnes, the head of wireless talks at the BBC, the section whose first director had been Matheson. The department was short of production staff: would she be willing to apply? (Guy Burgess had resigned from the unit in March to take up a post at the Foreign Office, from where he would embark on a parallel career as a Soviet spy.) Her interview took place on 2 June 1944, the Friday before D-Day. An internal memo sent by one of the 'solemn-faced-looking BBC gentlemen', as Goldie remembered the panel, read, rather dampeningly, 'Yesterday's appointments board was disappointing. There were only three possibles . . . We recommend Mrs Wyndham Goldie as our first choice.' The Board of Trade released her, reluctantly, and soon she moved into Burgess's old office at Broadcasting House, where she was quickly pursued by a note from the librarian hoping that she would be better behaved than her predecessor in returning books. (There is a footnote to this tale: Burgess's missing library books were hand-delivered back to the BBC by an unknown person on 15 September 1951. He and Donald Maclean had disappeared that May, and it would later transpire that they had defected to Moscow. The return of the books was duly discussed – in inimitable BBC fashion – through exchange of memo, with advice that the Foreign Office should be informed of this potential clue to the Cambridge spy's whereabouts.)

The war, according to Goldie's reminiscences, had pushed the talks department somewhat to the periphery. Unlike the department of Matheson's day, which had forged the beginnings of wireless journalism, talks now existed several removes from the news division, which was 'something on a pedestal way way away'. Suggesting a journalist for a talk was tantamount to suggesting a pornographer, she recalled. Still, it was enjoyable work, and she was good at it – she produced, for example, a landmark series on atomic power with contributors including Bertrand Russell, Jacob Bronowksi, J. B. Priestley and Group Captain Leonard Cheshire, the only British observer to have seen, from an American air force B-29, the bomb fall on Nagasaki.

And so in 1947, when the young television service tried to lure her from her comfortable office overlooking Portland Place, she was reluctant. On 14 May 1948, evidently in response to a refusal based on her horror of the working conditions, Collins wrote, 'I am just not going to accept no for an answer . . . I cannot help feeling that somehow or other we must have scared you off unnecessarily . . . the Alexandra Palace is very far from a dark satanic mill and . . . producers flourish quite heartily.' The anxiety continued: another letter from Collins dated 28 June begins, 'I gather that you are still worried because you fear that as soon as we have you at the Alexandra Palace we shall begin flogging you into an early grave.' But by then the deal was done: she would join the television talks department headed by Mary Adams, a BBC intellectual trained in genetics who had earlier employed the exiled Ludwig Koch and would later also hire the young David Attenborough.

It is hard, now, to recapture just how marginal and eccentric television seemed from the purview of the established wireless operation in its elegant (though war-battered) headquarters in Portland Place. Begun in 1936 as the first regular television service in the world, it had been halted for the duration of the war. Even by the time of Goldie's election-results programme in 1950, television transmitters covered only a fraction of the country. A 1951 article in the *Manchester Guardian* marked the austerity-slow march north of these magnificently alien objects by describing the freshly completed mast at Holme Moss in the High Peak: 'The giant stays which hold it, tethered to their concrete bases, stride away between the banks of the black moss for all the world like one of Wells's Martian machines arrested in mid-career.' Sets were the preserve of the well-off. In 1947 Goldie could comfortably reach millions with her work in radio. With television, maybe 20,000 households, all within a 35-mile radius of Alexandra Palace. The view offered to Goldie by the BBC's head of education Mary Somerville (another pioneering woman, who had unusually managed to keep her job in the BBC in the 1920s after having had a child), was typical: 'Television won't last. It's a flash in the pan.' Only a few observers, such as Harold Nicolson, saw as early as 1939 that television 'may alter the whole basis of democracy'. William Haley, the post-war director general – a 'shy, awkward' man, she remembered – was 'hostile to communication by vision at all; rather like Sir John Reith he thought it in some peculiar way immoral'.

The very geography of the operation was eloquent: Broadcasting House sat at the centre of establishment London, near Oxford Circus; television was on the margins of the city – a two-hour commute by bus, tube and bus again from Goldie's Kensington home. 'Sound was the father figure, established and responsible, television was

Alexandra Palace: 'gaunt and enormous . . .
derelict, mouldering, draughty'

the spendthrift and tiresome adolescent,' she recalled in *Facing the Nation*. 'I found that my office would be a tiny attic room reached by going into the open air in the rain and the wind, past the mouldering statues of Alexandra Palace; that it had no window, only a skylight; that it was warmed by a spluttering gas fire.' She continued, 'I often wondered whether I had been mad to change the civilised decorum of Broadcasting House for an existence which frequently seemed intolerable, which meant working late into the night in underground film-cutting rooms at the back of Alexandra Palace, returning along interminable dark corridors with an escort carrying an electric torch to keep off the rats and then, wearily, taking an infrequent bus down the hill to the underground station at Wood Green.'

None the less Goldie had the qualities, in this new career embarked upon in mid-life, to forge the future of television in ways are still being played out today. She brought a fearsome rigour, armfuls of programme ideas and, crucially, the political shrewdness to allow her to navigate – and dominate – the BBC's byzantine power structures. Most of all, she could see what the technology could do; she could see beyond the prevailing BBC view of television that, in her words, held that 'pantomime horses and chorus girls were its natural ingredients; it was not suitable for news or current affairs'. Goldie's overriding achievement was to prove that TV could tackle serious subjects and engage with the complexities of politics.

BBC news was, in the immediate post-war years under Tahu Hole, conservative and resistant to innovation, with a safety-first attitude that its own correspondents often found deadening and frustrating. Furthermore, Hole had no real interest in developing television news as a visual form, resisting even putting newsreaders on screen until weeks before ITN launched in 1955. But that created an opportunity for Goldie, who began to forge a current-affairs unit within Adams's talks department. An early example of her work was a programme called *Foreign Correspondent*, a series of films about post-war European cities. Unlike newsreel films, in which the pictures were paramount and a commentary was written over the top afterwards, the idea was to get the reporter, Chester Wilmot, and cameraman, Charles de Jaeger, to create a piece of reportage together in which words and pictures dynamically complemented each other. These were years of intense hard work. Adams wrote in her annual report dated 7 November 1949: 'She brings a much needed breath of the outside world and her knowledge of public affairs and personalities is a great asset . . . Her work here is carried out under conditions of great strain and difficulty and only persons of exceptionally good physical and mental health can survive it.' Everything was made up as they went along, all the skills of the current-affairs television professional invented from scratch: 'There was nobody ready-made. There were no commentators, no anchormen, there were no people in journalism who were accustomed to writing film commentaries.' Goldie found talent and trained people rigorously. In particular, she swept up a number of sharp, charismatic former MPs who had lost their seats in the 1950 and 1951 elections, among them Aidan Crawley, Christopher Mayhew and John Freeman.

She summoned up Gormenghastian images when recalling these years. Fellow producers 'looked like zombies . . . they were going about in a sort of coma of fatigue'. Alexandra Palace itself was 'a gaunt and enormous building on the top of a hill . . . it was derelict, mouldering, draughty, away from the centre of London . . . [a] huge, vast, rat-ridden building'. Collins and McGivern, the heads of the television service, had offices 'upstairs in a tower. Very much in the tower. There's a tiny tower which stands on the top of this huge building, up which you could climb precariously.' The gallery in Studio A, from which she would preside over programmes, 'was a creaking wooden platform . . . There was an iron ladder which you had to climb which was extremely dangerous so that . . . I had a special handbag made for me which I would hang over my shoulders because I had to hang on to both sides of this ladder . . . and many a secretary fell down this ladder to the detriment of her ankles.'

In 1953, Adams retired as the head of the talks department. Goldie made an application for the job, marked with a friendly handwritten note from her departing boss: 'I am glad to forward this.' Goldie's pitch began, 'The five years I have spent in television have been hard. They have been occupied, not only with building up new techniques of presentation in the talks field, but also with the training of personnel and the creation of a unit of production to deal with one section of talks output. That work is scarcely complete . . .' She did not get the job; instead Leonard Miall, until then a foreign correspondent – with no experience of television but a great knowledge of international affairs – was appointed, Goldie becoming his deputy. 'He was a nice chap and it worked roughly,' she later said, somewhat evasively. His subsequent annual reports on her work are glowing, with the occasional telling detail. 'She is quick to show her intolerance of what she regards as second rate. This keeps the department's standards high, but it sometimes tends temporarily to undermine the self-confidence of producers,' he wrote in 1956.

In 1954, Goldie moved with the talks department away from Alexandra Palace to Lime Grove in west London, a warren of slummy offices and studios with a faintly renegade air that was to be the home of BBC current affairs until the 1990s. The arrival of ITN in 1955 seriously raised the game for television news, with its unstuffy, buccaneering approach. Alasdair Milne remembered in his memoir, 'Everybody thought BBC Television News, under Tahu Hole's guidance, pathetic. ITN was winning the audience's appreciation hands down by its fresh and open approach, fronted by new faces such as Robin Day and Ludovic Kennedy, compared with BBC News Division's stiff and solemn demeanour.' That year Goldie was put in charge of the flagging *Panorama*, which had begun two years previously as a magazine programme with a kind of bouquet of contrasting items. Goldie decided it needed a complete reinvention as a serious forum for debating the matters of national importance. She relaunched it with her protégé Michael Peacock as editor, and Richard Dimbleby – who in 1953 had famously commented on the coronation – as its anchor.

Panorama was, she remembered in *Facing the Nation*, 'the voice of authority'. But now she went on to help invent what she called 'the voice of the people' – the current-affairs show *Tonight*. The programme, which ran five times a week from 1957 to 1965, a relatively short period that belies its influence and impact, was an invention to fill what was called the Toddlers' Truce – a gap in the early-evening schedule in which parents were supposed to persuade their children to go to bed. This now eccentric-seeming convention was swept aside by ITV, for which the shutdown merely represented a lost opportunity for making money.

Various ideas had been put forward by other producers to fill the gap, none of them up to snuff, as far as Goldie was concerned. She, meantime, was 'in great cahoots' with two mercurially talented young producers, Donald Baverstock and Milne. They had been discussing ideas for 'a new sort of programme . . . Donald's approach to his audience and to television was becoming very obvious, very individual and very clear. It was that *Panorama* was far too authoritative . . . He didn't like people being told things. He wanted to look at life through the eyes of the individual who was on the receiving end.' Goldie put forward the idea for *Tonight* – 'a magazine programme that would go on nightly . . . and be much more individual and human' than *Panorama*. McGivern was inexplicably angry and dismissive of the idea, initially – she realised later that his hostility was because of the acute shortage of television studios, for this was before the building of Television Centre. With Milne and Baverstock 'cooking up ideas for this programme very busily' she put her mind to solving the studio problem. Ever resourceful and willing to improvise, she remembered a place she had once visited to judge some BBC training-school exercises – a small space in Kensington that Marconi had established to train technical staff for the arrival of independent television. Goldie got her way. The programme was presented by Cliff Michelmore. The team included Jonathan Miller, who performed a weekly satirical sketch; Antony Jay, who went on to write *Yes, Minister*, and Alan Whicker. It 'looked at those in power from the point of view of the powerless', she wrote. '*Tonight* was . . . not rebellious, far less revolutionary, but it was sceptical.' Jay remembered it like this: 'We shared the feeling . . . that there was an out-of-touch group of people running Britain and covering their failures with a cloak of government statements and PR half-truths . . . abetted by docile and amenable Fleet Street proprietors who were worried about their advertising, and that we had a duty to show the other side . . .'

The files of programme correspondence show how controversial *Tonight* could be – there was an almost endless stream of letters from the town clerk of Nuneaton, for example, in autumn 1957, taking exception to a film on the town that had been, according to a memo written by Miall, deliberately 'sardonically humorous and unfair'. (A provocative report – for example referring to Nuneaton's most famous daughter, George Eliot, as a 'bloke' – had been made with the express purpose of provoking a reaction from townspeople that would be recorded for a second film.) The town clerk demanded that the mayor be interviewed to respond to this traducing of Nuneaton's reputation – they were not, he wrote, prepared to be judged by reference to 'slag heaps, rubbish tips and back alleys'.

The matter politely rumbled on for a year, being gently dribbled by the BBC into ever longer grass. The final round of correspondence came in 1958, replying to a suggestion from the unfortunate town clerk that a *Tonight* film crew should visit to report on a mobile X-ray unit being presented to the town by 'His Worship the Mayor', the kind of worthy event that *Tonight* would never have touched. The BBC reply delivered the polite death blow: 'Owing to arrangements caused by the General Election, TONIGHT is coming off the air as from the end of this week until 12 October, and so I am afraid it will not be possible for us to fall in with your particular suggestion, but I am sending it on to our News Services, both National and Regional, asking them to give it sympathetic considera-tion.' And there, to adopt the parlance of BBC memo-randa, the matter rested.

Goldie was a talent-spotter par excellence – largely of clever young men, though she also had clever young women on her team, including Catherine Dove, who became a producer on *Panorama*, and Cynthia Judah, later Kee, who ran the cultural side of *Tonight*. Many of those who began under her aegis rose to high power: Milne became director general; Baverstock controller of BBC1; Huw Wheldon managing director of BBC Television. She often said that her directors needed to have the instant reactions of a fighter pilot. Most of them had indeed served in the war, Baverstock ('a man of huge talent . . . wild and aberrant' in the words of David Attenborough) as a navigator for bombers. *Tonight* exemplified a new spirit in television, and its makers became the progenitors of other hugely significant programmes. The *Tonight* team created *Monitor*, a kind of *Panorama* of the arts under Wheldon; *The Great War*, the pioneer of blockbuster history series; and *That Was The Week That Was*, the satire show that defied convention and for many defined the new spirit abroad in the 1960s.

Goldie was a BBC loyalist to the marrow. When she died, she left all her money to the BBC's hardship fund, and all her papers to the BBC archive – her letters to her husband revealing a quite different side to her, one of childlike affection and admiration. (Six days before he died, she wrote to him, 'You are so talented, you make me earthbound and obvious . . . I have felt like a little ugly duckling wondering why this bird of paradise should ever have loved me.') For the last two years of her career, from 1963 to 1965, she at last ascended to the level of head of talks and current affairs. But her retirement was blighted by a dispute over the level of her pension, during which she seemed to have threatened to 'expose' the BBC's behaviour. Various colleagues wrote in support of her to the then director general, Hugh Carleton Greene (brother of the more famous Graham). One pointed out that she would never have been swayed by the siren call of ITV (as were so many BBC employees in the 1950s), and no one would have dreamed of trying to tempt her there, either – it would have been like trying to poach the director general. Kenneth Adam, then the director of television, paid tribute to her vast creativity. The BBC, he wrote, would be 'supremely unimportant without people such as Grace Wyndham Goldie'. He tried to excuse her rancour by reference to her relationship with the bottle – hardly an exclusive one, for this was the era of the well-stocked entertainments trolley and the office cocktail cabinet. We must take into account, he wrote, 'the knowledge we have of Mrs Goldie's reaction, in circumstances of entertainment, to her own job and that of the BBC'. (Only a BBC executive, one feels, would be quite so adept at euphemistically communicating that she could be bitter when drunk.)

Her biographer John Grist, who worked as a producer under her (and indeed had been an RAF pilot in the war) wrote that 'she could charm and frighten any man' and that within her there was 'a deeply set sliver of nastiness' that caused her to bully those she saw as vulnerable or inadequate. Melvyn Bragg told me he remembered a woman who was 'very clever, very tough-minded, and completely charismatic. She would perch on a stool in the bar and hold court, and toughies like Alasdair Milne and Tony Jay and even Attenborough and all the rest of them would just wait our turn to talk to Grace Wyndham Goldie. She knew what she wanted. She had a very good eye for young people who were talented; she had a very good eye for what would make a programme. Grace was quite somebody.'

It is hard, at this distance, to shake out the responses to Goldie. She was clearly an object of fascination as a powerful woman, an exotic creature within the BBC, described in terms subtly different from those employed to assess her male peers. The language used in relation to her quivers with male anxieties about females with power; and she herself clearly adopted strategies for inhabiting a senior role that rendered her unpleasant, at times, to her colleagues. Like many a baron of the BBC, she was not exactly a candidate for canonisation; but rather a professional broadcaster of immense dedication and rigour, whose contribution to the development of television – both in her early recognition of its formal possibilities, and in her realisation that it could handle politics and power seriously – was vast.

She was a very different person from Hilda Matheson, and was operating in a much bigger, more stratified and less bohemian organisation, and yet they shared this: a deep-rooted and idealistic belief in the civic purpose of broadcasting. Woodrow Wyatt, *Panorama*'s roving reporter in the late 1950s, wrote in 1985 that she 'should have been made director general of the BBC. She would have been another Reith, gentler and more tolerant but firm on quality and impartiality. She was the last senior official of the BBC who cared deeply about impartiality and insisted on having it. No one was allowed to slant, right, left, or liberal, in the programmes she controlled . . . She could have run the BBC far better than any of Reith's successors, and would have left a modern ethos behind her . . . The prejudice against women was, and is, nearly insurmountable.'

PART TWO

SLINGS AND ARROWS

5

The Great, the Good and the Damned

It was 30 June 1938, John Reith's last night as the founding director general of the BBC. There was no dinner, no ceremony. He had forbidden staff contributions towards a present and vetoed speeches. Instead, with a couple of colleagues, he drove up to the Midlands, to the high-power transmitter at Droitwich. He fulfilled the nightly task of shutting down one of its oil engines with his own hands – with his engineer's training, no one had to show him how to do it. Then he went on to Daventry, to the other great transmitter, which he had inaugurated a dozen years earlier. As night faded to dawn, he watched as the mast lights dimmed.

'A new day was breaking for Daventry and the BBC. In it I was nothing and nobody to Daventry and the BBC,' he recalled in his autobiography, *Into the Wind*. Then he drove back to Broadcasting House, arriving at 6.45 a.m. In his diary he recorded, 'Went to my room to collect the last of my gear and that's the end of that.' The flatness of it all is somehow unbearable.

He left the BBC in a mood of frustration, convinced he had not been fully stretched, clear in his view that television was a waste of time. (He called the opening night of the service in 1936 'a ridiculous affair . . . I was infuriated by the stuff they put out.') He went on to run another youthful projector of the glories of the British empire, Imperial Airways, and longed for a task of great responsibility during the war, but he believed Winston Churchill's hostility – they had fallen out over the BBC's coverage of the General Strike – stunted his career.

Being director general of the BBC rarely ends well, even when there has not been a metaphorical execution, as in the case of George Entwistle (resigned in 2012 after 54 days), Greg Dyke (forced out in 2004 after clashing with the Labour government) and Alasdair Milne (cast out in 1987 by the Thatcher-appointed Marmaduke Hussey). For those who have left as younger men, it has been hard to find their career's second act: like being prime minister, nothing quite equals it for power and glamour.

Dyke left surrounded by his own news crews and employees waving 'Save Greg' placards, finding out, or so he imagined, 'what it was like to be an American presidential candidate or Madonna'. John Birt (director general 1992–2000) wrote in his memoir, *The Harder Path*, that when he re-entered ordinary life, 'I had to learn how to use a cash machine, how to cope with the horrors of helplines, how to navigate London by bus and tube'. Entwistle, the Lady Jane Grey of the dynasty, announced his resignation while standing outside New Broadcasting House, just as he had done when he was proclaimed DG. He spoke in a clear but somehow faintly disconnected fashion, as if reading the lines of a play, 'I have decided that the honourable thing to do is to step down from the post of director general'. He then collected his overcoat and went home to his son's eighteenth birthday. He had spent twenty years stitching together his BBC career; it took 54 days as DG to unravel it.

Since the BBC's beginnings in 1922 the sixteen directors general have been men; Rona Fairhead became the first woman chairman in 2014. Reith was the longest-serving DG; none has managed more than his sixteen years. Bright boys, from solidly middle-class or aspirant working-class backgrounds, good grammar schools, academically suc-cessful: that has been the prevailing pattern. Tony Hall, DG at the time of writing, was absolutely typical: the son of a Birkenhead bank manager, he studied politics, phil-osophy and economics at Oxford. The BBC has always been the natural home of the meritocratic middlefolk of Britain, rather than the upper classes. Reith himself, though a son of the manse, was not deemed suitable material for university and resented it. In his autobiography he de-scribed his engineer's apprenticeship tersely: 'For four and a half years rising at 4.45 a.m., travelling from the west to the east end of Glasgow, a 56-hour week in the locomotive shops. For much of the time evening classes from 7 p.m. to 10 p.m.' His austere gaze was schooled there. 'When I presented myself at the shops it was with a ferocity of countenance designed to advertise a *nemo me impune lacessit* [nobody harms me with impunity] admonition.' His memoirs are strewn with schoolboy Latin, as if he is still a man with something to prove intellectually.

Directors general are often defined against the characteristics that have been seen to attach most strongly to their predecessor. Therefore Michael Check-land (1987–92) was importantly an accountant and not a programme-maker, as Milne was characterised as a brilliant programme-maker who had not understood money. Birt was marked as the outsider who could shake up the BBC and reform it, drag it forth from its complacent ways. Dyke (2000–2004), though another outsider, was seen as warm-hearted and egalitarian, 'full of emotional and spiritual generosity', according to Mark Damazer, who was deputy head of news under him; the man with the human touch to soothe the wounds caused by Birt's machete slashes through the corporation; the one to reconnect it with its creativity.

According to Sir Christopher Bland, the chair of the BBC in the last days of Birt and the appointer of Dyke, 'One's a roundhead and one's a cavalier. If you could clone the right characteristics of both of them you'd wind up with the perfect director general.' Mark Thompson (2004–12) was clever, strategic and thick-skinned; the supreme operator, big-brained and full of schemes and deals and politicking. Entwistle was, according to Professor Jean Seaton, the BBC's official historian, 'chosen incredibly particularly to not be a grand planner, to be a man that came in on the tube, to be straightforward, to be creative'. And where Entwistle – at least with the benefit of hindsight – was seen to have been lacking in experience, the DG at the time of writing, Hall, was the old hand – unbesmirched by the crises that toppled Entwistle but a battleworn BBC man to the bone, having worked his way through the corporation over thirty years, from trainee to director of news under Birt. At the same time, by virtue of having worked at the Royal Opera House for a decade,

Hall was deemed capable of understanding what the BBC projects to those outside the citadel – and of reconnecting it with its creative roots.

Like the aristocrats of ancient Rome, who revered the *imagines maiorum*, the wax masks of their forefathers that hung in the atria of their mansions, directors general need to invoke the right ancestor figures. (Traditionally, each departing director general sat for his portrait as they left, which would be placed in the council chamber in Old Broadcasting House. In tune with the times, these are now to be replaced by cheaper photographic portraits; and there are no plans for George Entwistle's image to hang among them.) After Entwistle's fall, there were many BBC old hands who glanced back at the control and order of Birt's regime with a certain wistfulness. James Purnell (he was head of BBC corporate planning under Birt, then Labour culture secretary, and later returned to Hall's BBC as head of digital and strategy) conjured Birt's shade: 'We have been here before,' he wrote in the *Financial Times* in 2012, referring to the embattled BBC of the late-1980s. 'The BBC was saved by Lord Birt's boldness.'

Looking back over ninety years of BBC history, it is Reith and Birt who now seem to loom largest as the BBC's most powerful ancestor spirits. Reith, the founding father, built it up from 36,000 licences to 8.7 million, from four employees to four thousand, from start-up to national institution, forging the ideals at its heart. Birt wrestled it into a post-Thatcherite shape, devised a digital strategy that is still being played out, and introduced sweeping reforms to its news operation.

Both trained as engineers. Both have lent words to the English language, neither – like their inheritances – unambiguous: 'Reithian' conveys all that is lofty in broadcasting, but comes with an atmosphere of puritanism and paternalism, of Auntie-Beeb-knows-best; 'Birtism', notwithstanding its rehabilitation as an idea, with its overtones of control and strategic farsightedness, suggests almost totalitarian levels of managerialism. Cognates include Birtspeak (convoluted workplace jargon, often expressed by 'croak-voiced Daleks', as the writer Dennis Potter memorably described Birt and Hussey, in his bilious MacTaggart lecture of 1993), and Birtistas, the cadre of loyal shock troops.

It was Reith's great achievement to shape the pragmatic decisions that went into the creation of the BBC into an ideology, which he outlined in *Broadcast Over Britain*. The BBC's powers as an educative tool were sketched out ('to have exploited so great a scientific invention for the purpose and pursuit of "entertainment" alone would have been a prostitution of its powers and an insult to the character and intelligence of the people'). It was activated as an equalising, democratic force: 'It carries direct information on a hundred subjects to innumerable men and women who will after a short time be in a position to make up their own minds on many matters of vital moment.' (Reith importantly invoked women, newly enfranchised.) 'The whole service . . . may be taken as the expression of a new and better relationship between man and man,' he wrote, a wonderfully hopeful thing to say. Its purpose was, he declared, to carry 'the best of everything into the greatest number of homes'. This ringing statement has been refined and rethought over the years – as in Huw Wheldon's formulation about making the good popular and the popular good. As a founding idea, it lies deep in the BBC's psyche. Hall himself referred to it in his first speech as DG in October 2013: 'At the core of the BBC's role is something very simple, very democratic and very important – to bring the best to everyone,' he said.

Reith was a complex person: as a father, he was distant; as an employer, terrifying. He was given to sometimes obsessional, one-sided relationships with younger women, and, as a young man, with his friend Charles Bowser, whom he clearly adored ('very good-looking and awfully pretty eyes,' he told his diary). Richard Lambert, at the *Listener*, recalled that when one met him in the corridor of Broadcasting House, 'he would look through you . . . like a dowager duchess meeting a chimney sweep in her boudoir'. Whenever he received a summons to Reith's office, 'I had to go apart for a minute in order to control my heartbeats and allow the mist which rose up in my brain to clear away'. Once inside, there was a strict hierarchy of spatial arrangements: 'a hard solitary chair for nobodies, or offenders; an upholstered armchair for senior subordinates or persons of standing; and a sofa, reserved for high dignitaries, or for individuals whom the interviewer wished to impress by close personal proximity'. When interviewed for his job by Reith, wrote Lambert, the first question was: 'Do you accept the fundamental teachings of Jesus Christ?' (Lambert made appropriate and unspecific noises.) Reith, all six foot six inches of him, strode about his office as he conducted the conversation. 'He reminded me somehow of a giant bird, moving restlessly and jerkily on its perch.' Like many in the 1930s, Reith had a weakness for a strong, Continental leader. He admired Hitler's efficiency and, in November 1935, noted in his diary that he had told Guglielmo Marconi that 'I had always admired Mussolini immensely and I had constantly hailed him as the outstanding example of accomplishing high democratic purpose by means which, though not democratic, were the only possible ones.' Reith is the single most significant figure in the history of the BBC, but by no means a wholly reassuring one.

I arranged to meet Lord Birt in the House of Lords. When he met me at the peers' entrance I was momentarily flustered – a tall man, he none the less seemed to materialise silently behind me – and when, after walking a great distance through the corridors of the Lords, we reached the room he had reserved, a resplendent chamber decked in elaborate Pugin wallpaper, I realised I could not find my digital recorder. Birt politely but firmly instructed me: 'Be systematic. Empty your handbag.' He might as well have asked me to remove my clothes as turn out that intimate cavern of scuffed paperbacks, topless Biros, dubious tissues and worse. But it struck me that this is precisely the approach he has adopted in professional life; and if it seems a bathetically domestic metaphor, then he himself in his own memoir twice described his work at London Weekend Television (LWT) – where he worked before the BBC – as 'tidying the drawer'.

Birt was born into a working-class family in 1944 and raised in Bootle and Formby; his autobiography conjures a world of whippets and terriers, football and redtops, polished doorknobs and scrubbed front doorsteps. He was educated a Catholic, was a bouncer at an early Beatles concert, and was the first member of his family to study at university when he went up to Oxford in 1963.

At Oxford, he was, by his own account, an unenthusiastic student of engineering. He fell in love with a glamorous American art student who would become his first wife, and became entranced by the cinema. He made an experimental film called *The Little Donkey* – in which a young man, having been taunted by various vampish and virginal women, turns into a toy donkey when a girl begins to touch him. '*The Little Donkey* was not an enduring masterpiece,' he acknowledged in his autobiography. But he had worked out what really caught his imagination – and it was not thermodynamics. After Oxford, he became a trainee at Granada, where, at twenty-two, he persuaded Mick Jagger, fresh from the quashing of a drug conviction, to be flown by helicopter into the grounds of a stately home to join a *World in Action* discussion about youth culture with a row of besuited establishment figures.

He moved to LWT and rose through the ranks, via its high-end current affairs programme *Weekend World*, to become director of programmes – having also taken leave to produce the famous interviews of the former US president Richard Nixon by David Frost. He operated at LWT in a labour-relations 'war zone' that made him 'hard-hearted about unionism', he recalled in his memoir. Restrictive practices and crew sizes grew. Despite his instinctive belief that the trades union movement was a progressive force, the TV unions were, he concluded, 'destructive . . . greedy for money, frustrating creativity, raising costs and reducing the number of programmes made'. As he prepared to join the BBC, he had, he wrote, 'become a convert to the value of markets, while maintaining a strong commitment to public service. I was hostile to vested interests. I had fostered my instinctive desire for reform and improvement, for tidying the drawer . . .'

If the BBC is in some ways a metonym for Britain itself, the tribally Labourite Birt – who would end up as strategy adviser to Tony Blair – was now ready to put it through a bloody, Thatcher-tinged process of marketisation and reform. You could see him as a kind of perfect personification of Blairism.

The stakes were high, Birt said. We were sitting at a dark-wood Gothic table. In front of him he precisely aligned his pen with a blank sheet of House of Lords writing paper. Politicians on both sides of the house 'had the evidence of their own eyes' that there were efficiency problems: the crews that turned up to film them were vast, he said. 'The BBC was wasting the public's money on a massive scale.' In his memoir, he called the BBC 'a vast organisation with no governing brain or nervous system, which had expanded and grown and multiplied organically . . . [it] was unmanaged and undisciplined in a way I would not, from the outside, have thought possible.'

Most important, he told me, 'the Tory right was on the march. Plainly we had a rarity: instead of having a government of the centre left or a centre right we had a

John Birt: He had 'an absolutist cast of mind',
according to one former colleague.

government of the right, and there was a strong group of
people on the right of the Conservative party who had real
free-market conviction that the BBC was too dominant.
There was nobody, as far as I know, who ever wanted to
abandon the BBC and see it disappear, but they did want
to see it massively reduced in size. And they were a strong
and confident government with a big majority.'

Margaret Thatcher, with her 'huge capacity for work and fantastic intelligence network' was 'really well informed and really interested in' the BBC – much more engaged than either John Major or Blair, he said. 'Although I was subsequently to meet every prime minister, generally one on one, in Number 10, she was the one who sought you out and wanted to have a dialogue and a debate with you,' he added. He found her 'radically minded, but by temperament much more cautious and careful than many of her advisers'.

He continued, 'I think what happened at the BBC made it easier for her not to do anything. In other words the introduction of Producer Choice [the BBC's internal market], the radicalism of that, the fact that ten thousand people left the BBC or were made redundant – plainly the BBC was taking efficiency seriously. That was only one of the things on her agenda – only one – but because one thing had been taken very seriously, I think that satisfied her radical urge.' He added, 'I'm not saying it was as devious and calculating as that makes it sound, but in general my view of such things is get ahead of the game. In other walks of life as well. Don't let things happen to you.'

Birt remains a deeply divisive figure. He was the man who walked the corridors with a clipboard silently taking notes before presenting his finding in bullet-pointed presentations; the man who employed phalanxes of management consultants and swat teams of accountants; who commissioned paper after paper on every issue to which his gaze swerved. He presided over the rise of the focus group, of branding, of concept-pitching, of distended pay for those at the top. In this way the internal travails of the BBC were a mirror for the times: similar changes were occurring in all parts of British life. Through Producer Choice the costs of many in-house BBC services, such as the record library and pronunciation unit, were made plain to programme-makers. Those units that did not offer value for money were allowed to wither. Costs were cut, and treasured outfits such as the BBC's radiophonic workshop – that radical locus for electronic music and experimental sound design – closed down. It was Birt's belief that, from greater efficiency, better programmes would inevitably flow.

At the same time, the 1990 Broadcasting Act meant that 25 per cent of programmes would have to be made by the independent sector. Producers left the corporation and sold back their programmes: Peter Bazalgette was given the popular show *Food and Drink* to make independently. Broadcasters who had started out as public servants were transformed into entrepreneurs. They forged small businesses that sometimes became very big businesses indeed. Fortunes were made. Often these production companies were eventually subsumed into the giant, international independents we know today. The BBC's culture – and the culture of the country – changed irreversibly.

There are those who say Birt saved the BBC. One of his achievements was without doubt an early embrace of the possibilities of digital – and persuading the government of the necessity of funding it. In contrast to the early directors general who had only barely, or only reluctantly, foreseen the importance of television, Birt grasped early that BBC online could and should be of vast importance to the corporation. The launch of BBC iPlayer itself might have lain over seven years ahead, but Birt anticipated in 1999, in his last speech as DG, that the future would be one of on-demand TV services; that great power would be held by those who control the 'gateways' into the digital world; that the BBC's audiences would want services on demand and on the move. On his watch, the BBC had established its website and by 1999 was already publishing three hundred stories a day on it, way ahead of most other news organisations, many of whom still regarded the Internet with suspicion. Bland summed up Birt's qualities: 'He is very determined. Very analytical. Good grasp of technology. Very good at handling the board of governors, at handling the interface of government and Whitehall. Thoroughly numerate.'

According to an old friend and colleague of Birt, 'He has an amazing capacity to get to the bottom of things and to work out how the engine works. His ability to diagnose a situation and to identify the fault lines and the weaknesses in it is considerable. He will dig, dig, dig until he gets to the thing.' The journalist and Labour peer Joan Bakewell said drily, 'I've always thought he was very good at joining the pipes. He structured the BBC like a piece of central heating.'

But there are plenty who believe that the BBC could have been reformed without Birt's approach of outpacing Thatcher – or, as he put it when we spoke, 'drawing the sting'. Sir John Tusa, who ran the World Service from 1986 to 1993 and then served as a newsreader in the mid-1990s, made a speech in 1993 in which he spoke of a 'climate of fear' at the BBC: you were either for Birt's reforms or against; the *ancien régime* had been discredited in its entirety; morale was pitifully low. The public-service ethos of the BBC was being savagely and carelessly dismembered. Potter, in his MacTaggart lecture delivered that same year, spoke of the 'fear and loathing' that swirled 'jugular high' at Birt's BBC. His was a vicious *tour d'horizon* without a hint of nostalgia, for he also remembered the 1960s when 'there was a bureaucrat in every cupboard and smugness waiting with a practised simper on the far side of every door'. But the sin of Birt's regime was 'management culture'. 'Management of what? Management for what? Management. Management. Management. The word sticks in one's interface,' he said.

Remembering the period, Tusa said, 'It's incredibly dangerous to have somebody leading an organisation whose first starting point is that he disapproves of all the values of the organisation. It doesn't work, and it didn't work. People went into a sort of internal exile, or a state of internal resistance . . . I don't say that he was a totalitarian, but I think he had an absolutist cast of mind.'

Birt's inability to find the language to bring the BBC with him was his failing, many of those around him felt. Grade put it bluntly in his autobiography: 'More charm in the train announcer's voice at Victoria.' Bland was kinder, telling me, 'John was unlucky enough to be Olympian in his style. His great weakness is, was, that he could never embrace the people who make the BBC what it is and make them feel loved and valued. He just didn't have the knack, whereas Greg [Dyke] had it in spades.' Even those sympathetic to him felt that though he could talk privately with passion and understanding about the creative process of programme-making, he lacked a warm and inspiring public rhetoric. A former senior executive recalled, 'There is a real dichotomy, because I think he was both a great DG and a disastrous manager. I think strategically he was remarkable. There's no doubt about it, he dragged the BBC kicking and screaming into the late twentieth century . . . I just don't think the BBC would have recognised the importance of digital without John.' But by the end of Birt's reign, there was an almost expressionistic sense of research papers piling on top of research papers, said the executive. 'He sometimes took far too long to take decisions, I mean to the extent that you would be tearing your hair out. So you'd do a paper on something and he'd say, "That's a very good thing, now the next iteration . . ." What you wanted was a decision, whereas he wanted process, you had to constantly do this process of more and more evidence, more and more evidence.'

One morning in 2014 I waited outside the office of the incumbent director general, Tony Hall. The panopticon-like New Broadcasting House in Portland Place, London, which had opened the previous year, was designed without offices with individual executives, but Hall insisted on having one when he arrived from his previous job running the Royal Opera House. As he came out to greet me he gestured darkly to the spot where Entwistle's reign had disintegrated, at a desk indistinguishable from those allotted to the junior ranks, in the full glare of open plan. Inside Hall's glazed lair – improvised from a meeting room – was a glass table on which lay his spectacles case and iPad (no computers for ranking BBC execs). It was surrounded by seats rescued from an old kitchen, and next to a window stood a pair of swivel chairs salvaged from Television Centre, which looked as if they might once have done service on a chat show. Hall described this recycling unprompted, perhaps keen to convey an impression of parsimony. On the wall was a series of photographs that I recognised as images from an old advertising campaign for the Royal Opera House, showing stars from the ballet and opera photographed in dramatic landscapes.

We settled ourselves into the swivel chairs. The BBC, said Hall, 'is Britain's voice, both to the world but also to ourselves. If you look, for example, at what is happening in local media, although we've been criticised for killing off local newspapers, when I go round local radio stations and regional television stations, and I see what is being done, we are reflecting parts of Britain to itself in a way that others simply do not do. So that is hugely important from the point of democratic debate.' The BBC is, he added, a kind of mirror through which Britain reflects itself to the world and the world to itself. Or a port: a conduit through which influences depart and arrive:

I love ports because they're very open, they're places where different currents and different ideas come together; that's what makes them so exciting and so inventive . . . I think the original view of inform, educate,

109

entertain is right, but now through a lens of what we're doing for Britain and the UK. And in truth, when I started off in the BBC, the counter-arguments about the BBC, which is that you're huge and you are 40 per cent or more of media revenues in this country – well we're now 25 per cent and if you look to the Googles and the Amazons and all the non-British firms that control our media usage, the BBC becomes more important, not less.

The frame of reference is changing, and the BBC must be more focused, he says:

I think we are at the end of a period of, as it were, unbridled expansion of the BBC. We're now in a period when we have to define much, much more carefully what it is the BBC offers and what it is the BBC can do, and recognise that we have to spend our money carefully, and around our priorities. That is why arts matter, our music coverage matters – I want those to be things you recognise in the BBC, up there with news. Drama matters. I think we have to be more constrained in terms of our ambition.

When Hall and I spoke about leadership, we discussed whether one person was capable of being at the head of the city-state that is the BBC – both as editor of that deluge of content, and its chief executive – or whether the role ought to be split. He pointed out the obvious fact that 'you can't be across all the output'. (Even the early DGs could

Tony Hall: 'We are at the end of a period
of unbridled expansion of the BBC.'

barely have been, certainly once the Empire Service, the
precursor of the World Service, got going in the 1930s.)
'In extremis, being editor-in-chief means this runs or
doesn't run,' he said. But more generally 'it means that you
have to think about the quality of your drama, the quality
of your music, the quality of your radio services, the
quality of your local radio stations. That's how I take
editor-in-chief. You are a one-person quality control.'

Being DG is also importantly about setting the tone,
about selecting the rhetoric. 'I for example want things
that are bold and feel that we're really pushing boundaries,
I don't want things which are safe and dull and placid, I
really do want things that make you feel, "bloody hell, the

Hugh Carleton Greene: DG 1960–69 and 'psychological warrior'
(portrait by Ruskin Spear)

BBC did that, that's fantastic" . . . I'm spending at least a day a week out with programme-makers because I feel they're the important, the frontline troops, the people that matter, the people that make the decisions and have the ideas that people pay their licence fee for,' said Hall.

As we spoke, I realised that Hall's office was filled with images of his predecessors. Its glass walls were imprinted with oversize, multiple portraits of the first director general: I counted eight giant Reiths bearing ferociously down on him. On a wall was a painting of Sir Hugh Carleton Greene, director general 1960–69, which once hung with the others in the council chamber. Hall said that he used to find it comforting when he was called in for 'a bollocking' by the board when he was the BBC's head of news. This is the image that Hall has chosen – this is the ancestor he has elected as his own.

Greene, like Reith and Birt, was a giant of a man, at almost six foot six inches. His portrait shows him sitting, in genially informal pose, on a high stool, his right hand in his pocket. He is slightly stooped, as very tall people often are, and just a touch crumpled. The painting conveys a faint loucheness – quite different, in fact, from Hall, who exudes the kind of reassuring, polite formality one might associate with a family solicitor or dentist.

Hall's most obvious intellectual ancestor is in fact his former boss Birt. It was Birt who plucked him from the ranks to take control of BBC television news at the age of just thirty-six. It was under Birt that he acquired the reputation of being the older man's 'head prefect', an ultraloyalist prepared to take on the painful and unpopular task of reforming the BBC's newsroom. But in his admiration of Greene he is attempting to connect with the more creative part of himself, the part that he has brought with him from the Royal Opera House. Greene's BBC was defiantly modern: his was the era of BBC2, *Z-Cars*, *Doctor Who* and the deference-slaying satirical show *That Was The Week That Was*. 'I wanted to open the windows and dissipate the ivory-tower stuffiness which still clung to some parts of the BBC,' Greene wrote in his book *The Third Floor*. 'I wanted to encourage enterprise and the taking of risks. I wanted to make the BBC a place where talent of all sorts, however unconventional, was recognised and nurtured, where talented people would work and, if they wished, take their talents elsewhere, sometimes coming back again to enrich the organisation from which they had started.'

Greene is, in the words of BBC historian Jean Seaton, 'the broadcaster's broadcaster. But the absolute key thing about Greene was that he was what I'd call an amphibian. He was that generation of men who had worked in government during the war'. Greene, the son of the headmaster of Berkhamsted School, began his career as a reporter. As head of the *Telegraph*'s Berlin bureau, he was the last British journalist to leave the city before the war. After being called up to the air force, where he became an intelligence officer, he was seconded to the BBC to work in German-language propaganda broadcasting. He described his role as 'deceiving, taunting but most of all and most important of all giving the enemy hard news even of our defeats, so that when, as one hoped, the time came for victories, they would believe what we said'. He wrote, 'To a German audience used to the most unscrupulous lies from its own press and radio we had to put ourselves across as strange beings who were really interested in truth even when the truth was, as it continued to be for many, many months, almost entirely to our apparent disadvantage.'

He had lived through a great deal. Speaking on *Desert Island Discs*, he recalled liberated Dachau: 'There was an incinerator, a big hall piled with corpses round an enormous stove and the notice was up in this big hall saying "*Reinlichkeit ist hier Pflicht, bitte Hände waschen*" – cleanliness is a duty here, please wash your hands. But the living skeletons in their striped pyjamas were in some way more difficult to bear than the dead. To have them kissing one's hands, embracing one . . .' Later, after the end of the war, he returned to the shattered Germany to help rebuild broadcasting there. These were the kind of experiences that made the travails of the BBC fall into some perspective when he became director general.

'To be director-general of the BBC is a very interesting experience,' he wrote in 1969. 'I doubt whether there is a more fascinating job in the world. One must be an editor with a feeling for news. One has to have a knowledge of the arts . . . One must be an administrator. One may be the father of 23,000 people. One must know enough about engineering to be able to ask the right questions . . . One must be able to walk with confidence in the political corridors of power . . . And one is an inheritor of a tradition of truthfulness and reliability which leads people at home and in nearly every country of the world to turn to the BBC in times of trouble.' Greene was an operator, a politician. Early in his tenure he had to face the government's Pilkington Committee on the future of broadcasting. He ran the BBC's campaign like a propaganda offensive: the case was meticulously researched, the committee was lobbied, rival ITV's strengths and weaknesses were painstakingly assembled. It was 'an exercise in psychological warfare and I confess that I found my experience as head of psychological warfare in Malaya in 1947 extremely useful', he recalled, remembering one of his post-war government jobs, this time countering Chinese insurgents. The eventual report, published in 1962, tightened ITV regulation and strengthened the BBC, allowing it to launch its second, colour channel, and to launch its local radio network: a total victory.

Even Greene, though, could not stave off every assault. In the end, his confident 1960s BBC was seen to have run out of control. Looking back, he remembered his tenure thus:

I think the BBC's output during these years . . . has brought out into the open one of the great cleavages in our society. It is of course a cleavage which has always existed: cavaliers versus roundhead, Sir Toby Belch versus Malvolio, or however you may like to put it. But in these years was added to that the split between those who looked back to a largely imaginary golden age, to the imperial glories of Victorian England and hated the present, and those who accepted the present and found it in many ways more attractive than the past.

Harold Wilson felt the corporation must be tamed, and deemed arch-Tory Charles Hill, who had chaired the Independent Television Authority, the ITV regulator, the man for the job. Hill was appointed chairman of the BBC: it was, remembered David Attenborough, like putting Rommel in charge of the Eighth Army. Greene did not last long. 'He was as sacked as Alasdair Milne was sacked,' according to Seaton. 'Just not quite so brutally.' The BBC, remembered Marcia Williams, Wilson's right-hand woman, had been behaving 'in the spirit of the independent empire that they had preserved for themselves'. In the end, even psychological soldiery was no safeguard against downfall.

Directors general are potentates: as grand as Medicis, their territories stretching as far and wide as kings' domains, their armies battle-ready. But for all that, they are vulnerable creatures. A twist of a political dagger can destroy them. They are always subject to a higher power – the government. It is in the BBC's nature for its dictatorship to be tempered by assassination. Hall may revere Greene, but his end is a warning.

6

'A spot of bother'

It was in the brief interval between a board meeting and a governors' luncheon that Alasdair Milne, the director general of the BBC, was coolly deposed by the chairman, Marmaduke Hussey. Ros Sloboda, who was Milne's PA at the time, remembers that day – Thursday, 29 January 1987 – vividly:

> He came down from the board meeting and into my little office at Television Centre. 'Right,' he said, 'the chairman's asked to see me. I'll just pop in. Then I'm going straight to lunch, and afterwards I'll pick you up and we'll go back to Broadcasting House.' It must have been literally a minute later that he came back, and said, 'I've been fired.' I looked at him and I said, 'Don't be stupid.' And I laughed. And he said, 'I'm not being stupid, Ros, they've fired me. They made me sign a piece of paper saying that I'm resigning for personal reasons, because they told me if I didn't sign it, it would affect my BBC pension. I'm going home now.' And he picked up his briefcase and went.

When I met Sloboda she was in the guise of the smartly dressed, no-messing personal assistant to Michael Grade, a role she had fulfilled for nearly thirty years. She exuded the air of someone who had seen all of the creatures in the broadcasting zoo and had long since ceased to be amazed by their antics. Back in the 1980s she had been a skilled secretary who had worked her way up through the BBC ranks to the role of DG's secretary. She had worked in the BBC for twenty years, beginning as a young, green girl in 1960, typing contributors' contracts for *Housewives' Choice* under a superior secretary who 'wore white gloves and big hats'. She remembered smuggling wodges of spoiled drafts out of the building on her first day for fear that someone would go through her waste-paper basket to check up on her errors.

Sloboda recalled that after Milne had left the building, she wandered dazedly into the room where the directors and governors of the BBC were preparing to have lunch. Hussey read out a brief statement. She remembered, 'Not one of them said, "Chairman, just a moment, can we clarify? Alasdair's resigning? What are the personal reasons? What? Why didn't he tell his colleagues?" No one said a word. They all talked about where they were going on holiday. I found that quite . . .' She paused, then seemed to dismiss the possibility of finding the right word. 'It's the English way,' she concluded, drily. Milne, who was DG from 1982, died in 2014. He never came to terms with the manner of his dispatch.

There was, of course, much more to Milne's tenure than strife: TV and radio flourished, and most viewers' and listeners' experience of the BBC of the time is richer and deeper than the particular darkness that Sloboda recalls from within that lonely and 'massive, oak-panelled office on the third floor of Broadcasting House'. None the less, she recalls the incoming fire as having been pretty constant through Milne's four-year director-generalship, which was certainly one of the most turbulent in the BBC's history. There were the libel cases arising from a 1984 edition of *Panorama* called *Maggie's Militant Tendency*, which claimed that the Conservatives had been infiltrated by elements of the far right; and there was the time Special Branch raided the BBC Scotland HQ after an investigation into the secret spy satellite system Zircon. There was a consistent sense of hostility and pressure from the Conservative government, within which there were zealots who would have seen the BBC privatised. And there was Milne's increasingly poisoned relationship with his board of governors; after the untimely death of the BBC's chairman Stuart Young in 1986, a Thatcher-approved replacement, Hussey, was inserted to bring the BBC to heel.

Sloboda described it like this: 'It was that terrible feeling you get when you first come home with a baby, and you don't know what you're doing. Events just always ran away with themselves. We were never in control of anything. It was terrifying, it was awful, it was absolutely exhausting. It was dreadful, absolutely dreadful. I've never worked in anything like that before or since.' She told me that she'd recently had lunch with George Entwistle's former PA. 'And she was saying how awful it had been, and I said to her, "Just think, you had 54 days of it. I had four years of it." Something else was always about to happen.'

In truth, it has always been that way, to a greater or lesser degree. The BBC is a battlefield that can be grim and

Alasdair Milne at Television Centre. He was DG from 1982
until his defenestration in 1987.

dark and strewn with human wreckage. It is where the
British gather to fight their most vicious culture wars. The
BBC's particular and paradoxical relationship with
governments – funded as it is by a politically negotiated
charter, independent as it strives to be in its journalism –
has meant it is caught up in dynamics of high power to a

greater extent than any other British broadcaster. It has always ricocheted from trouble to trouble, and it has crisis in its bones, back to 1926 when it survived a dogfight with Churchill over its coverage of the General Strike. In 2004 its DG and chairman, Greg Dyke and Gavyn Davies, resigned after a battle over the claim, made on the *Today* programme, that the government had deliberately exaggerated the threat posed by Saddam Hussein's weaponry in the run-up to the Iraq war – a crisis that crushed the source of the story, the weapons expert Dr David Kelly, into the unthinkable bleakness of suicide.

For Milne the squall over a documentary about Northern Ireland in 1985 was emblematic. It was shortly after Thatcher had declared that the IRA should be denied 'the oxygen of publicity' – this was four years before the then home secretary, Douglas Hurd, would order a 'broadcast ban' on organisations believed to promote terrorism, meaning that for six years viewers and listeners heard actors voicing the words of Sinn Féin members. A *Sunday Times* journalist, having caught wind of a BBC documentary in which Martin McGuinness was to appear, asked the prime minister at a press conference how she would react if a broadcaster was planning to show an interview with a leading member of the IRA. She replied in unsurprisingly strong terms.

All hell broke loose: on 29 July Leon Brittan, the home secretary, wrote a furious letter to the BBC declaring that the programme should not air – though, naturally, he had not seen it. 'The BBC would be giving an immensely valuable platform to those who have evinced an ability, readiness and intention to murder indiscriminately its own viewers,' he wrote. Milne was in Finland at a conference, about to start a holiday in Sweden. In those days before instant communications, Sloboda remembers finding the telephone number of the night steamer from Helsinki to Stockholm, and organising a Tannoy announcement to summon him to the telephone. 'I said, "Alasdair, have you ever heard of a programme called *Real Lives*?" He said, "No." And I said, "Well, there's a spot of bother."'

The BBC governors called an emergency meeting. With Milne still in Sweden, and his deputy Michael Checkland at the helm, they decided to view the programme before transmission. This was against all custom and practice: the governors' stated role was to set the broad policy of the corporation rather than to interfere in executive decision-making. In declaring it should not be aired, they pushed staff into open rebellion, and a strike was called. Michael Grade, then the BBC's director of programmes, remembered in his memoir the reaction among BBC employees: 'We felt betrayed by the people who had been appointed to protect our independence: they had buckled in the face of a blatant attempt by the Thatcher government to censor the BBC.'

When Milne returned five days later, having taken the decision, surely unthinkable today, not to cut short his holiday, he told the governors the programme was transmittable with only minor changes, and that he planned to say so publicly. His position – open and bloody-minded defiance of the governors – was regarded by Young as 'a resignation statement or a firing statement', according to the minutes of what was clearly a thunderously ill-tempered board meeting.

The documentary was eventually aired on 16 October, with minor changes. As the *Guardian*'s Belfast correspondent pointed out at the time, the reality of the programme was rather different from the fantasy. 'It was . . . generally agreed that the film, although well made, contained nothing new,' wrote Paul Johnson rather quellingly of an early, unofficial screening rigged up on the pavement outside the BBC's Belfast HQ by 'enterprising journalists' who had filched a tape of the documentary. Nancy Banks-Smith wrote in her review of the programme, 'Inconceivable that anyone should want to blow its head off. It is a lovely, sad quiet thing.'

On the day following its official transmission *Guardian* columnist Hugo Young refused to believe that the matter had been decently settled by the fact of the broadcast, and wrote eloquently of the wounds the affair had opened. 'The episode remains an indelible disaster. It shows how numerous are the enemies of truth-telling, how dangerous is the governors' conception of their task and how vulnerable television is to special rules and pressures which get in the way of it doing its job. The film has been shown, but it leaves the fragile threads of the BBC's integrity all but broken,' he wrote.

The film has been broadcast again only once. I was allowed to view it only under supervision in the editorial policy office (the unit responsible for patrolling the ramparts of standards and balance in BBC programmes). Virtually free from editorialising or voiceover, *Real Lives: At the Edge of the Union* offers up two parallel lives, that of McGuinness and his Democratic Unionist opposite number, Gregory Campbell, in long, uninterrupted interviews. What is striking is the sophistication and confidence of producer Paul Hamann's construction of the documentary; what is shocking is not that either subject might particularly advance his cause, but that each talks war and death amid utterly ordinary, and strikingly similar domestic existences – romping around on the beach with the kids, pouring milk from china jugs into cups of tea.

If one thing is certain about the BBC, then it is that crisis will always be around the corner. Its enemies are on the hunt, constantly – any mistake, any hesitation, and the predators pounce. From the outside, the corporation, despite decades of handling such moments, has frequently seemed uncertain and clumsy in managing them, often travelling from an initially sluggish response towards an exaggerated (though some might say ineffective) display of public self-laceration. One recently retired BBC employee deprecated, for example, the entire BBC culture of post-calamity enquiries. 'Was it a whopper of an editorial mistake?' she asked of the BBC's failure to pursue, in 2011, a *Newsnight* investigation into abuse allegations against Jimmy Savile. 'Yes, it clearly was a whopper of an editorial mistake. But you didn't need to spend £2 million and [hire] barristers and Nick Pollard [the former head of Sky News, who conducted an investigation] to uncover that.'

Hindsight is a wonderful thing. The events that led to the resignation of Entwistle as director general of the BBC on 11 November 2012 look fairly straightforward, from the outside and after the passage of years. A decision by the editors of *Newsnight* in December 2011 not to pursue allegations of sexual abuse against Savile led to the suggestion, in January 2012, that the BBC had conspired to drop the report to protect its Christmas tribute to the entertainer. Then, on 3 October, an ITV investigation into Savile was broadcast, prompting Entwistle to commission the report from Pollard into why *Newsnight* had stopped its own investigation. Separately, on 2 November, *Newsnight* broadcast claims by Steve Messham that, as a child in care in Wales in the 1980s, he had been sexually abused by a prominent political figure – a figure wrongly identified online, in the hours leading up to the broadcast, as the former chairman of the Conservative party, Lord McAlpine. This led to the spectacular departure of its DG after only 54 days in post.

All of that is easy to write: real life is not so simple. The crisis did not feel linear, like a row of dominoes. It was a complicated tapestry of events, in which a thread pulled loose in one part of the elaborate pattern affected the whole. Seemingly small decisions made by not terribly senior people had consequences that affected the entire corporation. According to Professor Charlie Beckett, founder of Polis, the journalism think tank at the London School of Economics, 'It was like a medieval medicine chart. The humours, the flows, were radically dysfunctional.'

But what if you were there? What did it feel like to try to survive the tempest as the waves crashed over your head? Much had changed since the 1980s. The pace of news had accelerated. There was the 24-hour news cycle: BBC executives at the centre of the Savile–McAlpine stories found their houses surrounded by reporters and cameras, feeding a ravenous monster that they themselves had reared. There was the echo chamber of Twitter: one of the catastrophes of the McAlpine story was that tweets started to appear before the screening of the report, causing speculation to coalesce around McAlpine as the probable public figure whom Messham had identified, mistakenly, as his past abuser. 'As soon as I saw that first tweet,' said one *Newsnight* staffer, 'I knew I'd lost my job.'

What was clear was that no one involved emerged unaffected. Two years on, there remained bitterness, damaged careers, deep feelings of injustice. Investigative reporters Liz MacKean and Meirion Jones, who had doggedly investigated Jimmy Savile's appalling abuse of young people in the first place, have been morally vindicated: there is now little doubt that, as Jones has written, 'Jimmy Savile was a predatory paedophile who had attacked many children in many locations.' The essential mistake was not to have run their journalism in the first place. But that notion was swamped as the BBC turned in on itself in the autumn of 2012. Accounts of what actually happened as the BBC attempted to contain the crisis – who was to blame, who did what to whom – differed sharply. All this was of course played out at a meta-level. No comparison could be made with the depth of trauma suffered by Savile's victims or those who had suffered abuse in children's homes. I spoke in detail to two people about the events inside the BBC in 2012 – not so as to provide a definitive account of what happened, or to apportion praise or blame, but to seek to express the lived experience of two individuals who had in different ways been caught up in the institutional crossfire.

Paddy Feeny was working in the press office at the time. Even on an ordinary day before the Savile crisis unfolded, he explained, the default position was of defence against endless incoming fire: 'Overnight there would have been anonymous BBC sources saying such-and-such an exec is a kiddy fiddler and such-and-such a journalist is an anti-Semite or whatever it was they were talking about that day. Plus 25 allegations of bias, plus a BBC presenter being arrested. All the usual kind of stuff.'

The morning would be spent 'agonising with people about what the accusations were, whether they were true and how and whether to defend them'. The afternoons, through to about 8.30 p.m., were devoted to fielding calls from papers; between 10.30 p.m. and midnight the calls would resume, after reporters had scoured each other's first editions. The whole cycle would begin again at about 6.30 a.m.

The normal quotidian business of dealing with reporters was a rough game. Feeny recalls one journalist who was 'personally vituperative, bullying, rude, stitched you up, never ever represented what you'd actually said to them'. Another, though working for a paper whose editorial line was hostile to the BBC, was 'in an odd way incredibly fair . . . They would call up and say, "So apparently somebody sneezed during the 8 p.m. radio news bulletin so obviously we're devoting pages four and five to why the BBC is spreading the plague", so you'd talk about that for a bit. And you knew perfectly well that it didn't really matter: you could have talked in Turkish for all the difference it would make. But you could sometimes say, "I am telling you emphatically, completely that is not true. No version of that is true. I'm not choosing my words carefully here because it's a little bit true. It's just not true," and that would be taken on board.'

The music modulated into a far darker key once the Savile crisis was in full swing. One of the grimmer aspects was the extent of the internal rancour it stirred up. According to one staff member who was embroiled in events, 'Everybody decided that they would take sides and take the opportunity to knife rivals or ex-lovers in the back.' On *Newsnight*, according to another, the sense was that 'when things did start to unravel the upper chain of management just disappeared, basically, and left the editor, Peter Rippon, to swing'.

The hangman was *Panorama*, by way of its investigation into *Newsnight*'s failings. This scenario – of one set of professionals spectacularising the errors of their own colleagues – is, on the one hand, admirable; on the other, disturbing. The journalists were all together, in glassy open plan, in New Broadcasting House, where they had just moved from White City. 'People from *Panorama* would be going through a script slagging off Helen Boaden and Steve Mitchell [the former director and deputy director of news], while Steve and Helen were literally in the next office having a meeting,' according to a *Newsnight* staffer. 'The way to save the BBC and the way to save *Newsnight* had become to get a rival programme to say how shit we were, and that was supposed to lance the boil. That was the cunning plan.'

In the opinion of the same employee, Rippon was virtually made a proxy for Savile by the press: 'Peter had his kids being followed while he was taking them to school. It was basically like he became Jimmy Savile.' 'Everyone on *Newsnight*', said Feeny, 'was exhausted and frightened and shouting. I have never seen so many tears.' He said of the *Panorama* report, 'I don't blame them at all. It was a good thing to have done. But they did take an enormous amount of pleasure in doing it in a slightly "we're-the-proper-journalists-around-here" way.' *Panorama* journalists passionately denied this: it had been done heavy-heartedly out of a sense of journalistic duty – and a premonition that their own careers would be unlikely to prosper as a result.

One *Newsnight*er remembers a colleague receiving a list of allegations from *Panorama* and 'just sobbing, saying, "My career is over."' 'But now I look back,' said the member of staff, 'I was a very junior producer on *Newsnight* when the David Kelly affair happened, and the fact was that there was a similar sang-froid within *Newsnight* about [the failings of] the *Today* programme.'

As the crisis moved into its final phase, the geometry of the press office's responsibilities became dizzyingly complex. Some of the team became caught up in the lengthy, and personally destabilising, matter of preparing evidence for the quasi-judicial process of the Pollard inquiry. 'I and others had their computer hard drives taken, had all their emails searched, lockers searched. I had to transcribe all my notebooks,' recalled Feeny. 'I had to provide a witness statement. I received a letter saying, "Go and find yourself a solicitor because you will need one when you are cross-examined."' In short: 'We were being investigated ourselves, and having to defend George Entwistle although he had effectively disappeared. We were promoting the *Newsnight* editor's version of events; dealing with the fact that other members of staff on *Newsnight* appeared to be anonymously briefing journalists every day that he was lying; and we were promoting *Panorama*, which was an investigation into why we were lying when we were defending *Newsnight*.'

The whole affair had not only been a crisis – but there had also been a failure to contain it. Instead of damping the flames, they had been fanned. Lord Burns, the chairman of Channel 4, who once ran the Treasury, said, 'It seemed to me to be symptomatic of what happens when somebody gets left holding the baby and doesn't quite know what to do and has nobody to turn to. When a crisis hits a poorly functioning organisation people run for the hills, because they don't want to be the person who's left holding the baby. But it is in those moments you actually need not only a good organisation but people who rise to the occasion, and who are able to work together, and who put their personal interests to one side.' It was in the context of this crisis over Savile that the second blow hit *Newsnight* – the wrongful naming on Twitter of Lord McAlpine as a child abuser, a claim made in relation to a separate *Newsnight* investigation. (The programme itself did not name the Conservative chairman.)

George Entwistle, the 54-day DG

These ugly days of fratricidal strife ended with the destruction of Entwistle, by John Humphrys on the *Today* programme. (Perhaps it is truer to say that Humphrys simply knotted a rope and handed it to his boss.) It was 10 November 2012, two days after the *Guardian* story establishing that Messham had been mistaken in believing that it was Lord McAlpine who had abused him. The interview was 15 minutes long, and an agonising listen. It ended at the point where Entwistle's very grip on language seemed to run out:

John, I am a director general who has encountered these problems and is doing everything, I'm doing, I am doing everything I can. I believe I am doing the right things. I know that there, that there, that there are times when I was thought to be being a bit slow over Savile. I could have been a bit quicker to move to announcing the, um, independent inquiries by a, by a few days, I, I, I've admitted that. But the truth is I am doing the right things to try and put this stuff straight. I am accountable to the [BBC] Trust in that endeavour. If they do not feel that I am doing the, er, the, er, right things then obviously I will, I will be bound, bound by their judgement.

What, indeed, of the Trust? It is in the nature of BBC rows to escalate quickly to question the very basis on which it is run. Some of the corporation's enemies clearly hold the view that if one undermines the foundations, the edifice might be more swiftly destroyed: like digging a mine in a medieval siege. In 2008 it took only a couple of weeks after Radio 2 broadcast prank phone calls by Jonathan Ross and Russell Brand to the actor Andrew Sachs, about Brand's having supposedly had sex with Sachs's granddaughter, for David Cameron, then in opposition, to forge the row into an argument about the BBC's lack of regulation and its 'squeezing and crushing of commercial competition'. (He was writing, strikingly, in Rupert Murdoch's *Sun*.)

BBC governance historically worked like this: from 1927, when the BBC became a corporation, the broadcaster was accountable to twelve independent governors, with a chair, who represented the interests of the audience, appointed the DG and set the broadcaster's strategy. But in 2007, after the Hutton report on the death of David

Kelly, the governors were replaced by the BBC Trust.

According to Lord Grade, the then chairman of the BBC who set the Trust's shape:

> What went before was highly unsatisfactory, because all the information that was necessary for the governors to make their decisions was edited, prepared and slanted by the management. They had no means of getting information themselves. And therefore all the investment decisions created a huge amount of suspicion that the management were trying to put one over on them . . . Management felt that the governors were a pain in the neck, and there was a lot of tension and conflict . . . and so I set about creating separation.

The Trust – which, unlike the old governing body, was set up as a separate organisation, with its own staff and premises – could act, explained one of its officials, 'to test rigorously any proposals from the BBC to get the tanks out of the garage and start heading off towards lawns. And it can carry out reviews of value for money, reviews of editorial standards.' But the question remained: was the distance of separation between the Trust and the executive set correctly? Was the Trust in fact in some ways simultaneously too close to the BBC and too distant? Was it possible for one person, the chair, to act both as cheerleader and regulator of the BBC? Did the governance structure contribute to the severity of the Savile crisis?

An alternative had been mooted before the Trust was adopted. Lord Burns had been commissioned by the then culture secretary, Tessa Jowell, to write a report on BBC governance. The suggested model was 'for the BBC to have a conventional board, with a non-executive chairman, a chief executive, a group of non-executive directors, and probably a small number of executive directors', explained Burns. 'And then there would be another organisation that would do the job of looking after the licence fee, a public-service broadcasting commission.'

There were some who remained attached to the view that the Burns model, or something similar, would have protected the BBC from the worst of the Savile–McAlpine crisis. When I visited Sir Christopher Bland, chairman of the BBC from 1996 to 2001, he said, 'I don't think the Trust is working. It's an unworkable model, because on the one hand it's asked to be separate and distinct from the BBC itself. The chairman is called the chairman of the BBC, but of course he's not. He's chairman of the BBC Trust, in a separate building, with separate staff, and no involvement in day-to-day decisions except on a post-hoc basis. But on the other hand, when things go wrong, the Trust is blamed for actions that are the responsibility of the executive.'

In Bland's view Entwistle 'would not have been fired and wouldn't have got himself into quite such a mess if he'd had a non-executive chairman to talk to . . . He couldn't ring up [chairman of the Trust] Chris Patten, still less walk into his office, and say, "Do you think I should go on the *Today* programme?"'

Bland had little time for Grade's arguments. 'I absolutely disagree with Michael Grade when he says there is not a problem with the structure. That's complete bollocks. That's Grade justifying the structure that he negotiated, put in place and then abandoned.' (Grade resigned as chairman of the BBC in November 2006 just before the Trust was due to take over from the governors.) Patten, who on 6 May 2014 announced his departure from the chairmanship after major heart surgery, was 'as good as you can be in that impossible job. I think he was unfairly reviled.' He remembered Patten telling him, 'I thought Hong Kong was difficult until I went to the BBC.' The former Conservative chairman, as the UK's last governor of Hong Kong, supervised its handover to the Chinese in 1997.

For his part, Grade said, 'The whole governance debate from beginning to end is crap, because governance is no substitute for judgement. I can cite you endless examples of plcs that had perfect governance and are no longer in existence.' In March 2015, though, Rona Fairhead indicated that a radical overhaul of BBC governance ought to be considered, suggesting a unitary board and an external regulator.

Lord Patten himself agreed that there have been difficulties of perception about the Trust's role, but he defended the principle – in public, at least. We met in his offices on Great Portland Street, five minutes' walk from New Broadcasting House, not long before he announced his resignation. 'One of our functions is of course to protect the independence of the BBC, and to stand up for the integrity of the BBC, and to expect the BBC to constantly surprise us by the way in which it meets its national obligation as part of this country's notion of civic humanism.

And to the extent that the BBC does that, I think we should cheer,' he said. 'But when it falls short of that I think we should say so. And that's partly about regulating, it's partly about openly challenging, and what we're trying to do after the last few years is to make the separation between the Trust and the executive more clear, which will sometimes mean that we step back from things that previously we might have got drawn into.' I asked him: do you think of the BBC as 'us' or 'them'? 'I don't want to be accused of heresy,' said Patten, 'but it's two in one.' He emphasised his points by tapping the desk in front of him with a plastic teaspoon.

I asked him whether he felt a closer relationship with Entwistle could have helped; did he know, for example, about the tweets on the morning of the *Newsnight* broadcast that contributed towards misidentifying McAlpine as a paedophile? Patten said he did know.

So why didn't he warn Entwistle?

It would I suppose have been open to me to phone up George Entwistle and say, 'Are you mad? Is this really serious?' If I'd done that, and George had intervened, and pulled the programme, the front pages the next day would have been: 'Ex-Tory chairman intervenes to stop *Newsnight* programme on ex-Tory treasurer.' It would have been regarded as a monstrous example of interfering in the BBC's editorial independence. What I did do was to phone up George and say, 'Are you sure that *Newsnight* is being properly run?'

And he didn't mention the tweets? 'No, because it seemed to me improbable that the director general of the BBC didn't know about something that everyone else was talking about.' Was Entwistle the right appointment? 'There was no reason for supposing that he would find the heat of Savile led to a sort of meltdown.'

Had he ever felt direct pressure from the government? Almost none, he said. 'But nothing had prepared me for the ubiquity of hostility in the press. When you have a newspaper saying that the latest script for *Sherlock* showed that the BBC is a left-wing conspiracy, you clutch at the air in desperation. When you see newspapers which have reported the infamy of the BBC five or six times as much as they've reported what President Assad is getting up to in Syria, then it makes you scream.'

How hard was it to run the BBC? 'Ten times more difficult than I thought it would be,' he said. 'I agreed to do it because I think it's a great national institution, it's an important part of our culture, because I have a romantic attachment to the things that the BBC has done at its best.'

I couldn't help wondering – especially in retrospect, after his heart problems became a matter of public record – just how far the difficulties of chairing the BBC Trust had worn him down. He had taken on the role through a romantic attachment to the societal virtues of the BBC, not, I felt, through any desire to take up arms in a cultural war zone. He was genial and gung-ho when we met, and occupied his large leather swivel chair with the full-bodied confidence of a tycoon. But all the while we spoke I could not stop summoning up his face as he stood next to the resigning Entwistle. In the film – mercilessly viewable on the BBC website – he chewed his lip distractedly. He looked haggard, forlorn, and very much alone.

7

Independent and Impartial?

'There is a brown fog; nobody is building; it is drizzling,' Virginia Woolf recorded in her diary of 6 May 1926.

> The first thing in the morning we stand at the window & watch the traffic in Southampton Row. This is incessant. Everyone is bicycling; motor cars are huddled up with extra people . . . It is all tedious & depressing, rather like waiting in a train outside a station. Rumours are passed round – that the gas would be cut off at 1 – false of course. One does not know what to do . . . A voice, rather commonplace & official, yet the only common voice left, wishes us good morning at 10. This is the voice of Britain, to which we can make no reply. The voice is very trivial, & only tells us that the Prince of Wales is coming back, that the London streets present an unprecedented spectacle.

Woolf was writing on the third day of the General Strike, observing events from her house in Bloomsbury. There were no newspapers but the hastily put-together government propaganda sheet, the *British Gazette*, edited from 11 Downing Street, and the TUC's the *British Worker*. Nearly 2 million workers, organised by the Trades Union Congress, had walked out in support of Britain's colliers, whose pay and conditions had been threatened by the mine owners. Leonard Woolf was running around organising a petition in favour of the strike; Virginia was worrying about frocks amid the mayhem; their well-connected friends were popping in and out, trading rumour and opinion. There was an atmosphere of national precariousness, the fomenters of the strike demonised by the establishment as Bolsheviks and revolutionaries, out to topple Britain. The previous autumn frightening rumours of fantastical plots (the guards at Buckingham Palace to be chloroformed, a soviet to be set up in the Palace of Westminster) were not discouraged by MI5 and Special Branch. There prevailed what we would now call a climate of fear. Woolf's dentist, whom she visited on 7 May, neatly articulated this sense of us against them: 'It is red rag versus Union Jack, Mrs Woolf.'

In 1926 the BBC was locked into agreements with the newspaper proprietors that there should be no news broadcast before 6 p.m., so as not to scoop the morning papers. Its bulletins were provided by wire services; the young company had no newsgathering operation of its own. But left as the main form of mass communication, the BBC assumed new importance. Immense pressure was placed on Reith to make BBC news 'a kind of off-shoot to [the *British Gazette*] . . . I was not going to have that at all,' he remembered in his diary. The following day, 5 May, he recalled, 'Churchill wants to commandeer the BBC.' The next morning, while Woolf was staring out of the window in Bloomsbury, he was rowing again in Whitehall: 'Winston . . . said it was monstrous not to use such an instrument [as broadcasting] to the best possible advantage.'

For the first time, the BBC carried news bulletins throughout the day. According to Woolf's account they were not especially earth-shattering. On 7 May she described the morning broadcast: '"London calling the British Isles. Good morning everyone." That is how it begins at 10. The only news is that the archbishops are conferring, & ask our prayers that they may be guided right. Whether this means action, we know not. We know nothing.'

The prime minister, the reassuring, tweed-clad Stanley Baldwin, adopted a subtler position than Churchill, his chancellor. A Cabinet meeting of 11 May, according to Reith's diary, took the view that the government should be able to say 'that they did not commandeer [the BBC], but they know that they can trust us not to be really impartial'. In other words, the government saw there were advantages in retaining at least the appearance of an independent BBC. By this time, Baldwin had broadcast to the nation from Reith's own home, heavily coached by him – Reith persuaded him to include the words: 'I am a man of peace. I am longing and working and praying for peace, but I will not surrender the safety and the security of the British Constitution.' When Ramsay MacDonald made a request to put an alternative point of view, as leader of the opposition, Reith consulted Baldwin, 'strongly recommending that they should allow it to be done'. The message came back that the government was 'quite against MacDonald broadcasting' – leaving Reith in, as he saw it, 'a very awkward and unfair position'. MacDonald did not broadcast. Reith had successfully fended off a takeover, and, insisting on broadcasting statements from the TUC, had prevented the BBC's becoming a mere propaganda tool. He had held on to the BBC's independence, just – but he had tactically sacrificed impartiality.

Later, Reith spoke of his stand on the General Strike as a triumph. Others were less certain. Hilda Matheson put it this way: 'The Government did not commandeer the BBC . . . It is no secret that it was owing to BBC insistence that the bulletins of the Trades Union Council, as well as the communiqués of the Government, were both broadcast. It is not suggested that the weight of the BBC was not thrown preponderatingly on the side of authority; the important point, for the social historian, is that a degree of independence and impartiality could be preserved at all.' Richard Lambert was rather more blunt: 'I have heard Sir John Reith many times express his pride in the part played by the BBC in supplying the public with "unbiased" news during the strike. But Labour circles received these boasts with scepticism; the only point of general agreement being that the cessation of newspapers during the strike had given broadcasting its first big opportunity of showing what it could do to influence a steady public opinion in a crisis.'

Reith had laid out the importance, and the difficulties, of impartiality for the young BBC in *Broadcast Over Britain*: 'So far controversial matters have rarely been handled by us, and if dealt with at all, usually in an innocuous manner. It has been considered wise policy up to the

present to refrain from controversies as a general principle
. . . the tendency is, however, in the direction of giving
greater freedom in this respect . . . It will not be easy to
persuade the public of an absolute impartiality but impartiality is essential.' The General Strike, the first great testing
ground for the BBC, showed how fragile its two great
founding principles of impartiality and independence
were in times of crisis or conflict with the government.

Nearly ninety years on, the same principles lie at the
heart of BBC news. Director general Tony Hall, who was
director of BBC news in the 1990s, put it like this: 'I think
the reason that the vast majority of people in this country
support the BBC is because we are independent, we are
impartial. That means we should be brave, we should
stand for good, honest journalism, brave journalism.' But
the question for BBC news is now, as it always has been,
how far those great principles – independence and impartiality – can withstand the pressures brought to bear upon
them. Moreover, what does impartiality actually mean in
practice?

BBC news and current affairs as it is in the twenty-first
century would be unimaginable to Reith, Matheson or
Lambert. In their day, news was a relatively unimportant
part of the BBC; now it dominates both the institution
itself and the UK news media. It is an empire within an
empire. It employs 8,000 of the corporation's 21,000 workforce, 5,500 of whom are journalists. Via the World Service
it has a tentacular reach to 191 million people across the
globe, and its presence on the domestic scene is overwhelming, with its TV and radio bulletins both national

and local, its website, its heavyweight current affairs shows such as *Newsnight* and *Panorama*. Eighty per cent of Britons receive their news from the BBC, and it is more trusted than any other news provider.

In this context of dominance, the relative attention the BBC gives to a story, or a point of view, matters enormously. By casting its powerful beam of attention on to a matter, it causes that story to become important, an issue of national moment; and other news organisations follow its lead. If it turns its gaze away, the issue can etiolate and fade from the public consciousness. How much time to devote to reflecting public anxiety about immigration? How much time to accommodate the views of those who deny climate change? In politics, this question of weighting is especially fraught and contested. How much time to devote to covering a colourful but marginal political party? What about airing the views of racists or terrorists? In February 1965, the then DG Hugh Carleton Greene, speaking by candlelight in a snowy Rome beset by power cuts, laid down what he believed were the limits on impartiality: 'Although in the day-to-day issues of public life the BBC tries to attain the highest standards of impartiality, there are some respects in which it is not neutral, unbiased or impartial. That is, where there are clashes for and against the basic moral values – truthfulness, justice, freedom, compassion, tolerance, for example. Nor do I believe that we should be impartial about certain things like racialism or extreme forms of political belief.' One BBC journalist put the problem of impartiality to me this way: 'You're in a pub and two men are having an argument. One is claiming that two and two are four. Another is claiming, with equal passion and conviction, that two and two are five. What do you say? That the truth lies somewhere between?'

Impartiality, then, is something of a moving target. And the stakes are high: if the BBC slips to the left or the right, it can take the whole nation with it. Politicians themselves care about BBC news and current affairs in a deeply personal way: it is a reflex of politicians (and indeed of newspaper executives) to calibrate their notion of the day's mood by the choice of items on the *Today* programme. In the hermetic world of the British establishment, a news programme's power may be judged by not how many are in its audience, but by who they are.

Free from commercial interests, lacking the baser instincts of newspapers or independent broadcasters who must satisfy the whims of proprietors and shift copies or sell advertising space; lacking, even, the kind of principle that animates the *Guardian*, which was founded explicitly as a progressive, justice-seeking voice in the wake of the Peterloo massacre, BBC news, theoretically at least, just *is*: ineffable, truth-telling, a kind of God the Father of journalism. Mark Damazer, the master of St Peter's College, Oxford, once the deputy director of BBC news, told me he believed that one of the BBC's functions was to 'hold the ring in the middle of a national debate'. Without the BBC performing that function, in the centre of news and current affairs, giving it an existence beyond the world of ulterior motives and the market, debate would become 'atomised', and 'I have an absolutely fundamental view that

Britain would not be the better for it, we'd be the worse for it,' he said.

Just as the nation's sense of itself can shift according to the BBC's news agenda, so the corporation can shake and founder because of decisions taken in its news and current-affairs division. The immense power that the BBC wields in reporting and reflecting the matters of the day is counterpointed by immense vulnerability. The BBC in turn knows that though it is free from the vagaries of funding by direct taxation, its charter and the level of the licence fee are set by the government of the day. Thus it is that the government and the BBC will always dance a curious dance together – a delicate waltz that might slide into a sparring match, a grapple or, occasionally, a death grip. The corporation's moments of greatest existential struggle with governments have tended to flow from arguments about news and current affairs, especially at times of conflict: first, the General Strike. Later, the Suez crisis, the Falklands, Northern Ireland, the Iraq war. It is no coincidence that every director general since the early 1980s (except for the accountant Michael Checkland in the late 1980s and the outsider Greg Dyke in the early 2000s) has passed through BBC news and current affairs, for it is the corporation's intellectual powerbase and producer of its most ambitious officer class. Tony Hall was director of news; George Entwistle edited *Newsnight*; Mark Thompson edited the *Nine o'Clock News* and *Panorama*; John Birt was deputy director general in charge of news and current affairs; Alasdair Milne was in at the birth of current-affairs programmes such as *Tonight*.

The last of these moments of great vulnerability came in 2003–4, as Britain went to war with Iraq. But the seeds of the story of the BBC's falling out with New Labour went back to the party's years in the wilderness, and resentment at what was regarded as the unfair treatment of former leader Neil Kinnock in the press. Under Blair, things would be different. They would not allow control of the narrative to drift away from them. 'There was a tremendous activist sense that they needed to be "on it" the whole time, with every weapon at their disposal – rhetorical, technological, persuasion, off-the-record chat – and they were probably as intense a set of media managers as we've had before or since,' remembered Damazer.

According to Richard Sambrook, who was the BBC's director of news from 2001, trouble between the BBC and New Labour was already brewing when Britain intervened in Kosovo in 1999: Alastair Campbell, Blair's press secretary, accused the media of being too much in thrall to Milošević's 'lie machine'. After 9/11, the stakes became much, much higher. Sambrook recalled:

There would be constant faxes complaining about bits of coverage. It came to a head after [reporter] Rageh Omaar had done a piece from Kabul about a hospital, or some casualties or something. Alastair rang me about 10.30 p.m. absolutely screaming down the phone saying words to the effect of: 'If you don't get this crap off the airways we're going to throw everything we've got at you.' About two days later Kabul fell so all that went away but, by that time, within Downing Street the notion was the BBC was not on side; that they're a problem.

Damazer – who spoke with the calming, judicious air of a diplomat – often had the job of responding to complaints: in a tone of relentless, public-service politeness, such that 'politeness became an *aesthetic*'. He added: 'I think what Campbell would say – there may be some truth in this – is that low-level attempts periodically to resolve difficulties with the BBC always met a maximalist response, even though I would say it was polite. The BBC is institutionally not merely not rude but almost painfully, almost aggressively polite . . . he may well have simply got irritated by hitting his hand into the blancmange and it just being a blancmange.' Damazer said that he became personally anaesthetised to the battering from Campbell and Co.: the New Labour commentary on impartiality was so obviously self-interested 'that you could only see it as at least in part an attempt at persuasion or coercion'.

The crux came at 6.07 a.m. on 29 May 2003, when Andrew Gilligan reported on the *Today* programme that, according to a source, the Joint Intelligence Committee report on Saddam Hussein's chemical and biological weapons capability had been 'sexed up' by the government to include a claim that such weapons could be activated within 45 minutes of an order. That there had been any deception was fiercely denied by the government, and it was amid the ensuing maelstrom that the man eventually revealed as the story's source, Ministry of Defence weapons expert Dr David Kelly, took his own life. Lord

Hutton's controversial and contested report into Kelly's death was deeply critical of the BBC and precipitated the resignation of both the director general, Greg Dyke, and the chairman, Gavyn Davies. That simultaneous toppling of the twin titans of the BBC was an unprecedentedly traumatic event in the history of the corporation. It was made all the more bitter by the fact that the struggle was fratricidal: Dyke's appointment as DG had been controversial because he had been a donor to New Labour, and an old friend and neighbour of the Blairs. It was a deeply shocking event: the national broadcaster's DG and chairman both brought down by a government from which it was supposedly independent, and a left-of-centre government at that. But it has always been foolish to assume that left-of-centre governments are more intrinsically sympathetic to the BBC than Conservative ones. Marcia Williams, in her memoir of working at Downing Street, had this to say about Harold Wilson's relations with the BBC, for example: 'It is untrue to say that Harold has an obsessive dislike for the BBC as a whole. He is exasperated by the bureaucracy . . . What he has often objected to, and will no doubt continue to do so, is the way it has been administratively run . . .' Hardly a ringing endorsement.

Looking back, it is Sambrook's view – one that would not be uncontested among his former colleagues, nor indeed among the dramatis personae of the Labour government – that 'what Kelly told Gilligan was right, was the right story. Unfortunately Gilligan was sloppy in the way he reported it, the *Today* programme was sloppy in the way they handled Gilligan and by the time the row was happening the BBC was at full defensive mode with its old tactic of "Let's put up a wall of defence and shelter behind it." But the mood within Downing Street was not going to put up with that.'

He continued, 'I suppose in a sense what I'm saying is that Kelly was a kind of mini-Edward Snowden story.' Sambrook was referring to the whistleblower who, in 2013, had provided the *Guardian* with information about US and UK government surveillance of phone and Internet connections, sparking a worldwide debate about surveillance and security. 'Kelly was saying that actually this intelligence has been completely misused, and many people inside the tent knew it and were uncomfortable about it. I think the BBC could have done it in a different way and in hindsight I regret that we didn't manage it properly. But if the BBC says to the government that fundamentally there is rot at the core here, that's a big problem. And the BBC has to be very, very careful because it is in the end dependent on a political deal to exist.'

Sambrook and I were talking over indifferent coffee in the faintly shabby bar at the top of the high-rise St George's hotel, next door to Broadcasting House. He left the BBC in 2010, and later became professor of journalism at the University of Cardiff, applying his mind to the academic study of the mechanics and ethics of news. He gazed distractedly out of the window, down on to the city far below. 'After Hutton, I'd say it was about two years till I got over it. It was the first thing I thought about when I woke up in the morning and the last thing I thought about when I went to bed at night, every single day. What happened there? What could I have done differently? To what extent was I culpable, or not culpable?'

He went on:

If Edward Snowden had contacted *Panorama* or *Newsnight* could they have done what the *Guardian* did? No. No, they couldn't. They might have been able to do a piece at a meta-level, a headline level, but they could not have done what the *Guardian* did with Snowden. I find it uncomfortable to say that but it's the truth.

So what does that tell you about the BBC? It tells you that in the end there is a limit to its independence – some would call that public accountability. It is a wonderful news organisation. It does fantastic journalism every day. But there is a limit to it. And I think in the end that was part of a miscalculation in the Kelly story. We thought we were genuinely independent. And we weren't.

Where does BBC journalism stand in the post-Hutton era? James Harding, the former *Times* editor who joined the BBC in August 2013 as head of news, took the opposite view from Sambrook. 'The BBC has over the years shown it is entirely independent. There are always debates about coverage. But the independence of the BBC and the BBC journalists I think is central to the public's trust in the BBC. That's the reason why it has the support it does,' he told me.

Nick Robinson, who was at ITV at the time of the Hutton inquiry, and who went on to become the BBC's political editor, was more optimistic than Sambrook when we spoke. Hutton 'didn't have the chilling effect it might have done', he said. He had never bought the idea, he said, that the BBC was 'being cowed'. Robert Peston, the BBC's economics editor, agreed: 'I have not felt haunted by Hutton,' he said. When he broke the story of the failure of the bank Northern Rock in 2007 – withstanding complaints from senior politicians, the Financial Services Authority and others 'who were claiming I was somehow out to destroy the British economy and I should be shut down' – he felt completely supported by the BBC.

Far more crushing, Robinson said, to the temper and spirit of BBC news had been the aftermath of the troubles at *Newsnight* – the Jimmy Savile and Lord McAlpine affairs and the resignation of George Entwistle. 'It produced an atmosphere of flatness at best and despair at worst. If organisations can be depressed, it was depressed. Our organisation stood accused first of suppressing a major story then of carelessly libelling a public figure.' The arrival of Hall and Harding had, he said, 'freed people from the introversion – until the next crisis rolls along, of course'.

When I visited Jeremy Bowen, the BBC Middle East editor, at home in London between trips to Syria in the violent spring of 2014, he fondly remembered Harding as a young reporter on the *Financial Times* who stayed on the couch in his room in the El Rancho hotel during 'a long stakeout' in Port-au-Prince in 1994. The point was: Harding had earned his spurs; he had done his time as a reporter in the field, Bowen felt. Harding himself told me, when we met in May 2014, that he was committed to investigative journalism: 'I think the issue with investigative journalism is that it takes a lot of time, real resources, and a lot of discipline in pursuing the story, addressing every angle, thinking it through. And we live in a world where there are quite a lot of litigious people. You've got to be able to take those pressures on.' Investigative journalism was, he said, 'one of the central roles in everything we do in current affairs. And should be true across all of our news output.' That summer, though, it was announced that the editor and deputy editor of *Panorama*, the BBC's flagship investigations show, would be leaving their roles, and shortly afterwards its four dedicated reporters were made redundant.

How far is the BBC willing to take its journalism up against the establishment – and the government, which in the end seals the BBC's fate? Others I spoke to within the BBC were much less confident than Harding. 'The BBC is at its highest levels concerned with not offending the establishment, not making enemies in important places. Its core purpose – independent and impartial journalism – clashes with its survival instincts, and that goes back to the beginning,' said one senior journalist who, in a time of job losses, asked not to be named.

Another took an even bleaker view: 'Newsgathering – covering the stuff that is happening in the world – we do that brilliantly. The BBC newsgathering operation is genuinely a wonder to perceive. But digging out original stories? No, sorry. Nor has it ever done. When push comes to shove, senior people at the BBC consider themselves part of the establishment.'

The journalist saw the problems at *Newsnight* – the failure to run Liz MacKean and Meirion Jones's investigation into sex-abuse allegations against Jimmy Savile, and the mistaken identification of Lord McAlpine on social media as a paedophile – as symptomatic of a bloated, anxious management, their timidity exacerbated by the fact that few had themselves worked as field producers or reporters. The employee called such managers, as well as the departments in charge of editorial policy and compliance, 'journalism deterrence squads' who were strangling the efforts of colleagues 'like Japanese knotweed'. Journalists were afraid of not being backed up by the BBC, added the employee, when the pressure was on – and compared the corporation's approach with the much more bullish, confident and 'cheeky, risk-taking' stance of *Channel 4 News*. 'The BBC always buckles, always folds. You feel that as a journalist, they will abandon you; if you take a risky story to them it's as if you are actively trying to get them into trouble. There is an institutionalised anxiety and mistrust.'

Peston, who started his career in newspapers, said, 'There is a risk-averse culture that means when the BBC wants people who can break stories it has to look to recruit from outside. When the BBC is training young journalists, it starts by telling them about the regulatory restraints: it starts with the rules and says, "Don't you dare break them."' Bowen paid tribute to an organisation 'in which there's a great deal of creativity, where programme-makers really believe in what they're doing, and in which people, despite everything, are proud to work'. But he, too, believed that the BBC was 'overly bureaucratic'. At times, he said, he has felt the BBC has 'lost sight of our core business, which is broadcasting. It's the British Broadcasting Corporation. It's not the British Management Corporation.' He added, 'I think things are changing, but we have also been too worried about what other people think, particularly the *Daily Mail*. There are times we could have, instead of apologising, stood up for ourselves a bit more strongly.'

A combination of anxiety and bureaucracy had led to some absurdities. As a senior correspondent of thirty years' standing, Bowen had, in 2013, been required to undertake an online multiple-choice training course, 'which had a scenario in which I was doing the morning shift on a local radio station in the Manchester area, and reports were coming in from the police of two Manchester United players involved in an incident in a nightclub'. He shook his head in disbelief. 'I could have been trying to find out what was going on in Syria while I was doing that. That's absolutely insane, that kind of stuff.'

I asked another senior journalist whether the BBC had moved to the right, as some would argue. There was laughter. 'Undoubtedly. You're not supposed to read the *Guardian* at the BBC, because it confirms everyone's prejudices. For years it has been more important at the BBC to be seen reading the *Telegraph* or *The Times*.' Peston agreed. The BBC is often characterised as having an institutional bias to the left, but, he said, 'What actually sends BBC news editors into a tizz is a splash in the *Telegraph* or the *Mail*, rather than one in the *Guardian*. Over time the criticism of the *Mail* and the *Telegraph* that we are too left-wing has got to us. So BBC editors feel under more pressure to follow up stories in the *Telegraph* and *Mail* than those in the *Guardian*.' He added, 'For example, for a long time I was saying that the phone-hacking scandal [pursued by the investigative reporter Nick Davies of the *Guardian*] was a huge story. Basically, I was talking to people who didn't want to hear. It took us a long time to get stuck in. The fact is that we don't get criticised for not following up the *Guardian*, but we do get criticised if we don't follow up the *Mail* or *Telegraph*. There is no institutionalised bias to the left – if anything, it is a bit the other way.'

I also wondered whether there was what Birt might have once called a bias against understanding in BBC news and current affairs: I was thinking of the almost invariably aggressive tone of its news interviewing. Being tough on politicians was one thing; assuming that allcomers were, to paraphrase Jeremy Paxman 'lying bastards lying to me' was, surely, deflating rather than aerating of debate. News interviews, especially political interviews or those with a strong streak of controversy in them, seemed to have become unhelpfully one-note, with subjects ironing out all subtlety in their answers in order to project their 'message' and interviewers interrupting them at every turn. Hall, when I discussed this notion with him, rejected it. 'We give the British public more of a platform to understand what's important in the world than any other broadcaster and it's one of our prime purposes. And you do that in all sorts of different ways and different styles,' he said. But Hall acknowledged the aftermath of his predecessor's reign. 'After the last two to three years the organisation's taken a real battering and I think it did at times lose its sense of confidence,' he said. 'I want to ensure that the BBC has got confidence to do great journalism, bold journalism and journalism that people admire.'

What was clear to me is that no other news organisation existed under the pressure that BBC news withstands. An honestly made mistake at a newspaper such as the *Financial Times* or *Telegraph*, or even at a broadcaster such as Sky or *Channel 4 News*, might lead to embarrassment. But the BBC, at the centre of our culture, funded by the public, has its own magnification effect. It is, as Hugh Carleton Greene put it as far back as 1969, 'the universal Aunt Sally of our day'. At the BBC, a mistake can lead to humiliation in the national press, to employees being doorstepped by newspapers, to questions in parliament, to multimillion-pound semi-judicial inquiries. The whole edifice can tremble; the well-being of the entire organisation can founder; its future funding can be imperilled.

Under such circumstances, it is no wonder that the BBC has often resembled a damaged, bullied child, defensive and afraid. The stakes for BBC news are immeasurably high. If we believe in the BBC as a beneficial ideological intervention in our lives, if we believe in it as the greatest, and best-loved, signifier of Britain there is, then things have to change – outside the BBC as well as inside it. The whole culture that surrounds it needs to become less vituperative, more mature. As one of the journalists I spoke to said, 'The fact is, you are more likely to be bullied if bullies think they can bully you.'

8

Enemies at the Gate

Some of the most outspoken critiques of the BBC come from within it. One cold sunny morning in early 2014 I visited Jeremy Paxman in his flat in west London. As he padded around in his socks, filling the cafetière, he railed against what he described as the BBC's 'closed corporate culture'. He said, 'It is smug. I love the BBC in many ways, but at the same time it has made me loathe aspects of it, and that's a very odd state of affairs. When I see people being given £1 million merely for walking out of the door' – he was referring to the payments made to executives such as former deputy director general Mark Byford, who was awarded £949,000 in 2011 – 'when I see £100 million being blown on that DMI [digital media initiative] thing, a stupid technical initiative like that, I start wondering: how much longer are we going to test the public's patience?' Not long after we spoke he resigned from anchoring *Newsnight*, after working on the show for 25 years, though he continued as a presenter of, among other shows, *University Challenge*. On another occasion a prominent BBC broadcaster railed passionately to me against the 'corruption' of management, who had 'helped themselves'. 'The BBC's greatest enemy', he said, 'is itself. They are handing people ammunition.'

It has been observed that the nearer one gets to the centre of the citadel of the BBC the easier it is to dislike aspects of it. According to Lord Burns, the chairman of Channel 4, 'I love the BBC. My life without it would be' – he paused, and said with great emphasis – 'terrible. But it is not an organisation that does very much to help itself: there is a strange situation where people love what the BBC does but the closer they get to the BBC the less attractive a place it seems.' Paxman, like many critics of the corporation I spoke to, told me he believed the corporation was too big:

There's a pile of stuff on the BBC I can't stand. My idea of hell is going down in one of the lifts in that ghastly new building [New Broadcasting House] in a lift which has Radio 1Xtra plumbed into it. I don't quite understand why the BBC does Radio 1Xtra, I don't really understand why it does Radio 1. Clearly, you can meet those needs commercially . . . the BBC has got an unfortunate history of never seeing an area of broadcasting, or increasingly a web presence, without feeling the need to get into it itself.

He went on:

There's no argument that the BBC distorts the marketplace in online [news]. Hugely distorts the marketplace. And one understands of course that the *Mail* and the Murdoch empire dislike a commercial rival which they are obliged to compete with on unfair terms. And I don't think that has been really sufficiently grasped at a senior level. It just happened, in the same way as has

the proliferation of extra television channels, the proliferation of extra radio channels – and, going further
back, the move into local radio. These things just
happened because the BBC is institutionally unable to
countenance something without wanting to have it for
itself . . . I don't tar Tony [Hall] with this because he
hasn't been there long enough, but the great smell that
comes off those pay-off scandals – and I think they are
scandals – is of an organisation which became complacent, preoccupied with the conditions of its senior staff,
at the expense of a strategic vision.

These were strong words from a star BBC presenter.
From outside the BBC, however, comes a chorus of much
more consistent and committed opponents of the corporation, many of whom husband their hatred of the BBC
with the kind of single-minded tenacity that makes
Paxman's outburst of frustration seem mild-mannered.

There are many variations, but the central objection to
the BBC, from which many related critiques flow, arises
from the fact that it is an intervention into the market,
with a historical tendency towards expansionism. Martin
Le Jeune, a free marketeer and a former director of public
affairs at Sky, wrote, for example, in a pamphlet for the
think tank Centre for Policy Studies: 'Far from being a
powerhouse of originality, the BBC is a persistent me-too
broadcaster with a serial record of imitation. Pirate radio
stations spawned first Radio 2 and then Radio 1. Sky News
brought forth BBC News 24 (virtually until the moment
of launch the BBC official line was that there was no need

for rolling news) . . . The BBC is too often a parasite on other's ideas to allow its claim of creative contribution to be taken at face value.' The reasons for this 'intellectual larceny', he posits, are both psychological (the BBC's un-flinching self-belief and sense of mission) and a matter of policy. Because the BBC is funded by a 'universal tax . . . it is under a corresponding obligation to seek to provide services of all kinds to all people'.

Also noted by critics is its paradoxical position as both a publicly funded civic organisation and, in the shape of its for-profit arm, Worldwide, an aggressive business that exploits its brand ruthlessly in the commercial world – and from a highly advantageous position financially. Pure free marketeers also object to it as a paternalistic organisation devoted to giving audiences what they 'need' (rather than what they want). The market, these critics argue, is an ex-cellent mechanism for matching broadcasting supply to broadcasting demand. Linked to that is an on-principle objection to the licence fee. By its critics this is seen as not only a regressive tax (everyone pays the same regardless of their means) but also intrinsically unfair, since one is obliged to pay it in order to watch anything on TV, even if one does not use the BBC's services. (One must also own a TV licence, incidentally, to be able to watch live-streamed material from 4OD and ITV Player as well as the BBC iPlayer, though viewing on-demand services was not, at the time of writing, subject to the ownership of a licence.) Licence-fee evaders were, at the time of writing, subject to prosecution, a sanction regarded by critics as overly draconian and a drain on the resources of magistrates' courts, though in September 2014 the culture secretary, Sajid Javid, announced a review into the law making non-payment a criminal offence.

Frequently appended to these overarching criticisms is the notion that the BBC, through its very constitution and nature, is unconsciously statist in outlook, a worldview that it inevitably reflects, especially its news coverage. Furthermore state funding and lack of a bottom line lead inevitably to complacency and an overgrown bureaucracy, it is argued – and in recent years to highly inflated pay deals at the top. According to Le Jeune, 'Anyone who has had to spend much time with its managers and numerous lobbyists struggles to remember [its] glorious record in the face of so much intellectual self-satisfaction and so little sense of obligation or accountability for the vast wealth which the BBC has.'

But such arguments hardly account for why passions against the BBC run so high. What fuels a loathing that seems for some to become almost a monomania? One of the most prominent critics of the BBC is the *Daily Mail*, which rages almost daily at the corporation, while simultaneously running avalanches of articles devoted to the clothing, diets and love affairs of the stars employed by it. Paul Dacre, the paper's editor, politely declined to be interviewed by me, but sent instead a copy of his 2007 Cudlipp lecture, which, he told me, still accurately represented his views on the BBC.

It made for arresting reading. He began with the traditional *Daily Mail* claim that the BBC is too big (the *Mail* has pretty consistently since the 1920s set itself against the monopolistic nature of the corporation, on principle and for reasons of commercial anxiety). From there, he quickly moved on to argue that the corporation exerts a kind of 'cultural Marxism'. This, he says, attempts to undermine 'the values of conservatism, with a small "c", which, I would argue, just happen to be the values held by millions of Britons'. He picked out for special mention what he saw as the BBC's pig-headedly liberal stance on immigration and Europe.

The corporation, he said, though it 'glories in being open-minded, is, in fact, a closed thought system operating a kind of Orwellian Newspeak . . . this, I would argue, is perverting political discourse and disenfranchising countless millions who don't subscribe to the BBC's worldview'. Thus, he argued, the BBC had been responsible for 'the current apathy over politics'. Even the greenish-centrist stance projected at the time of the lecture by David Cameron was, argued Dacre, a result of a kind of emasculation wrought by the BBC – a 'blood sacrifice to the BBC God'.

The word 'worldview' was key. The *Daily Mail*'s own worldview (and, to be fair, that of all newspapers, to a greater or lesser extent) is a fabrication, a jigsawing together of structural templates, stock narratives and character types. The *Daily Mail*'s worldview is especially seductive; it is bought into on a massive scale by the British public. If one were looking for the most internally consistent 'closed thought system' in the domestic media landscape, one would, surely, have to turn to the *Mail*. And if one actually believes that the *Daily Mail* offers a complete and accurate reflection of Britain as it really is, then no wonder that the BBC looks inadequate or out of step. But I also wondered whether there were something else afoot in this long-nursed enmity – consciously or not. The *Mail*, founded in 1896 by Lord Northcliffe, comes from the same era of mass communication that spawned the BBC. It was the *Mail* that saw some of the early potential of broadcasting: it sponsored Dame Nellie Melba's broadcast from the Marconi headquarters. The *Mail* and the BBC are sprung from the same time and the same set of historical conditions. Far-seeing Reith got it wrong when he wrote, in *Broadcast Over Britain*, 'Some prophets are foretelling a colossal struggle between the powerful Press interests and ourselves. I do not believe there need be any such thing.' There was a colossal struggle and, arguably, the *Mail* lost.

Dacre also claimed in the lecture that he would 'die in a ditch defending the BBC as a great civilising force' and would 'pay the licence fee just for Radio 4'. For the fact is that few principled BBC critics have cursed the corporation entirely out of existence. (Direct commercial rivals may be another thing: Christopher Bland, for example, is not alone in believing that Rupert Murdoch 'would be the happiest man in the world if the BBC were abolished, or, even better, if he were allowed to buy it'.)

There is a sense from a number of its critics that the BBC would be entirely tolerable – if only it would conform to one's own view of what it ought to be, a view often infused with a certain nostalgia about an older, better, half-remembered corporation; certainly one that was smaller, probably with Radio 4 at its heart. Quentin Letts, the *Daily Mail* columnist, whose articles are capable of boiling over with fury about the BBC, has, paradoxically, applied to be its director general, twice. Was he serious? Well yes, up to a point. 'I was so angry,' he told me in the canteen at the Palace of Westminster, where he is based as a parliamentary sketch writer. 'I saw all these bloody careerist lefties prospering at the Beeb, and I thought, "Why should they have it?" I mean some of those people are as nuttily left-wing as I am nuttily right-wing, and yet they all get bloody top executive jobs, and not a sniff of a rightie.' He smiled. There was something immensely disarming about his candour – though I wasn't sure that he had much evidence for the BBC's being full of 'lefties'. For example, in December 2014, one of the BBC's producers, also based in Westminster, made a high-profile departure to become director of communications of Ukip. And Letts himself had hardly been banished from Broadcasting House; he was the presenter of a successful series on Radio 4. 'I knew I didn't have a chance,' he added of his DG applications, 'but I thought, well, I'll try and make the point . . . complete failure!'

Margaret Thatcher, of course, looms large in the story of the BBC, as the avenging fury of the private sector, under whose premiership the door was opened to Murdoch's Sky, and in whose later, hawkish cabinets were those who would have seen the BBC privatised. She herself, according to her biographer Charles Moore, a former editor of the *Telegraph*, lacked the appetite to raze it. She disapproved of the licence fee in particular as a regressive tax, and the BBC in general as, in Moore's words, 'left-wing, monopolistic, anti-her'. She listened to the *Today* programme; Denis paced the ramparts to tell her how awful the rest of the BBC was. Coverage of Northern Ireland, the Falklands, and her contention that the BBC was grotesquely inefficient and overstaffed (based on personal observations of the BBC's turning up mob-handed to film her) provided the backdrop for an especially fraught and hostile period of the BBC's relations with the government. But as for destroying the BBC wholesale, Moore said, 'I think if you look at it politically it just probably wasn't worth the effort. It was useful politically to keep on attacking it, to take the wind out of its sails and make it try to examine itself and get a bit frightened.' He added, 'There was a strand in the BBC that she liked – a sort of high-minded public service broadcasting ethos – the daily service, covering state occasions, that kind of thing.'

I met Moore in a formal members' club in the City, all wood-panelling and discreetly attentive service. I had asked him to tell me about his time as a licence-fee 'martyr'. Softly and precisely spoken, he described his antipathy towards the licence fee, comparing it to

the tithes that the Church of England used to live off. Very much the same argument was advanced for them, which is that we are doing God's work – which is basically what the BBC says; it has broadly the same role in society as the Church used to. We're doing God's work, and so you've got to pay for it. And as with the licence fee so with the tithes. They (a) bore heavily on the people financially, and (b) they were being made to pay for beliefs that they didn't necessarily share. So they were keeping Archdeacon Grantly in a style to which he was accustomed, even if they were dissenters or atheists.

Moore reached the end of his tether, he said, in 2008 when presenter Jonathan Ross and comedian Russell Brand were heard on BBC Radio 2 leaving messages on actor Andrew Sachs's answering machine, joking that Brand had, in Ross's words, 'fucked your granddaughter'. 'I thought that this was an absolutely classic example of the sort of arrogance of power that organisations like the BBC get, where they think they can do what the hell they like. It seemed to me to be the BBC's credit crunch, the equivalent of the Royal Bank of Scotland, and for quite a similar reason: hubris. And I thought it was disgusting, a remarkably disgusting thing to do by Ross and Brand personally, but in a way even more disgusting that the BBC thought they should run it.' Moore particularly disliked that the whole thing was cloaked in humour. 'How did a public-service organisation think that its highest-paid person should be a sort of foul-mouthed comedian, and how could they think that they should pay him so much?' (Ross's contract was reportedly worth £6 million.) Moore decided not to pay his licence fee until both had left the BBC; eventually he went to court. 'I was hoping for more publicity on the day, but then Gordon Brown called the election.' He laughed.

I thought about Moore's remarks about Thatcher's tactical abrading of the BBC – pecking away at it, aggressively but gradually – when I encountered Rob Wilson, the Conservative MP for Reading East, who, in his single-minded pursuit of the organisation, had made a modest name for himself. We met in early 2014 in the canteen at Portcullis House, he – thickset, ruddy-faced and square-jawed – making an oddly Dickensian-looking couple with his lanky, pale, earnest researcher, who wore dark-rimmed hipster spectacles and took notes of our conversation. Between October 2012 and March 2014 the BBC Trust received 33 letters or emails from Wilson; the DG received 34 – or so I discovered by putting in my own freedom of information request. ('God knows what the cost of it is; and each one provides a kind of rent-a-quote for *The Times* or the *Sun* or whatever,' said the BBC's then chairman, Lord Patten, of Wilson's letter-writing.)

I wondered what Wilson's constituents made of it. 'The letters pretty much all deal with what I would regard as significant issues in the public interest,' he said. Was the BBC a route to a certain kind of fame, I wondered? Was it by adopting a role as the BBC's most vocal parliamentary critic that he had decided to try to make his name? 'It's certainly not about self-promotion, because there are lots of ways you can do that as an MP, and I wouldn't say the BBC is necessarily the easiest way to do that. But I mean if you've got strong opinions, why shouldn't you write to the BBC Trust?' Wilson had become the 'go-to' MP for journalists seeking a swift anti-BBC quote – though he said he turned down 50 per cent of requests for interviews.

The BBC had enormous culture problems, argued Wilson:

You could draw comparisons with the NHS, because the NHS has similar problems. Management don't like criticism, staff don't feel they can speak, change is very difficult to move through the organisation . . . the BBC has to make a decision about what it wants to be in the future, and with charter renewal coming up this is a good opportunity to do so. But the idea that it can just go on and on and on growing and stuffing people's wallets full of money at senior level is just not on. It just can't continue.

Wilson's analogy with the NHS began to niggle at me: I wondered whether there was a shared technique at work from the right: not to demand anything so radical as the eradication of either the health service or of the BBC, but to undermine them so that public trust might be gradually blunted. Towards the end of our interview, Ed Vaizey, the culture minister, happened to wander over. He asked me jovially, 'What are you doing talking to this right-wing loony?'

One of the more eloquent critics of the BBC was David Elstein – a veteran broadcaster who had begun his career as a trainee in the corporation. We met at a cafe local to his home in south London; he was leafing through the *New Yorker* and the *London Review of Books* as I arrived. The whole BBC structure was perverse, he told me; and its domination of Britons' news coverage simply bad for democracy. The BBC principle of universality – that it provides something for everyone, and everyone pays the same – was a false goal, he argued, a 'fraudulent piece of rhetoric' that existed only in order to justify the licence fee. A smaller licence fee to fund a central corpus of freely available public-service broadcasting would be fairer, he said, with subscription funding the rest and acting as an incentive to make better programmes – more like the 2013 Netflix remake of the 1990 BBC drama *House of Cards*, or indeed the BBC's own 2013 detective series *The Fall*, and less like the wildly popular *Sherlock*, starring Benedict Cumberbatch, which he regarded as 'hugely overpraised: juvenile and dismissive of the audience'.

The BBC, he said, caused him to feel a mixture of 'pride and frustration'. Pride because it was a bastion of British-ness at its best. Frustration that, despite its high level of public funding, it fell short of his expectations: 'I think the BBC is a fantastic institution, right up there with the monarchy, Parliament; it's less than a hundred years old and we have a collective identification with it. But on the other hand I feel frustration that it doesn't do better with such a powerful position. It does a lot of mediocre programming. Not bad programming, just mediocre programming.'

I was curious to know how Elstein had forged his views, and asked him about his family background. Both his parents, he told me, had been brought to Britain from Poland as orphans by the Rothschild Foundation. They had together run a ladies' outfitter's in Golders Green. A scholarship boy, he emerged from Cambridge University at nineteen with a double first in history and, in 1964, went straight to the BBC as a trainee. He later worked on *Panorama* and *The Money Programme*, and moved to senior positions at Thames, LWT and, later, Channel 5 and Sky, as well as working in independent production. He also applied for the director-generalship of the BBC in 1999, though he didn't get a final-round interview. But most of his first year at the BBC was spent on attachment to the newly founded Centre for Cultural Studies at Birmingham University, where sociologists Richard Hoggart and Stuart Hall were doing pioneering work. Hoggart had recently sat on the Pilkington Committee on the future of broadcasting, which had tightened regulation of commercial TV and paved the way for BBC2 and local radio. This was a formative experience: Elstein wrote a paper on the effects of mass media and a mini-thesis on public-service broadcasting. His views 'did not entirely please Richard'. By contrast with Hoggart, he found the Pilkington view of broadcasting 'oppressively paternalistic'.

Elstein's view that subscription should gradually take over from the licence fee was first aired in the 1980s. His disobliging views had caused him to be viewed as a prophet by some; by others as a broken record, harping on about his pet theories, disappointed not to have become DG, informed by his career working for the rivals of the BBC. There is perhaps something of a Cassandra about him: 'People occasionally mock me and say, "David, it's only been thirty years since you started this debate. How does it feel not to have succeeded so far?" . . . There's a whole parade of BBC executives, media academics and newspaper columnists who hold the licence fee as a kind of article of faith . . . it's become almost more important than the BBC itself, or public-service broadcasting itself, and I just feel mildly bewildered by it. It's just a funding mechanism; it has no moral significance.' Politically, he called himself a 'radical centrist', and said that he had voted for everyone from the Communists to the Conservatives, via the SDP. According to Lord Burns, 'I think that in the long term he is probably right about some things. David's problem, though, is that the way he puts his arguments is not designed to build an alliance.' Another broadcasting veteran said, 'He actually makes it quite difficult to agree with him: it doesn't matter how far you go towards him, he will always move himself so that he's at a more extreme position.'

Such heterodox thinking is as old as the BBC. Captain Peter Eckersley was one of the most significant figures in the early history of British broadcasting, and the BBC's first chief engineer. He was forced, however, to resign from the corporation in 1929 after it became clear he was having an affair with Dolly Clark, a singer and the estranged wife of BBC conductor and programme organiser Edward Clark. (An undated note in Eckersley's BBC personal file recounted that 'on one occasion they were more or less drunk together at a public dinner and the affair created a good deal of talk and scandal, which was used as an opportunity for effecting his departure'.) They married; and after Dolly met Hitler through Unity Mitford, they both became entangled with Oswald Mosley's fascists, and were enthusiastic pre-war tourists to Germany. But by the time war broke out the couple had separated. She, with her son James Clark, spent the war in Germany, working in the Reich's English-language radio unit, to which she recruited William Joyce ('Lord Haw-Haw'), notorious for his propaganda broadcasts. Eckersley, remaining in Britain, found his reputation tarnished and was turned down for war work.

All this lay far in the future though, when, in the years before the First World War, young Peter – a cousin of Aldous Huxley – was a schoolboy at Bedales (cold baths, wholesome food and adolescents 'completely unaware of the world's unreason'). He was a talented boy in a talented family – his younger brother Roger would go on to become director of programmes at the BBC and his elder brother Thomas was an accomplished physicist who also worked in the field of wireless. In his book *The Power Behind the Microphone* he remembered a formative event: one night he came home from school to find that Thomas had 'set up some experiments on high-frequency currents . . . I found our playroom filled with lovely and exciting experiments. There were induction coils to make fat sparks, Leyden jars, long black rods of ebonite wound with green silk-covered wire, X-ray tubes and galvanometers. The things, their touch and shape, gave me a sensual pleasure and made me want to understand what they were for.'

In 1906, still a schoolboy, he and a friend set up what they called Wavy Lodge in the school grounds – an old henhouse with benches set up for experiments to test the relative merits of different aerials. They would use wireless to relay the results of cricket matches to the school buildings from distant grounds, using a mobile transmitter carried about on a soapbox fitted with wheels from a perambulator. A decade later, he was a wireless equipment officer in the Royal Flying Corps, where the possibilities of the thermionic valve – which 'has the power to shrink the world to the compass of a living room' – were being explored. He was standing next to Major C. E. Prince, who had been a Marconi engineer since 1907, when Prince became the first person to speak by radio to an aeroplane pilot in flight. ('Hello, Ferdy. If you can hear me now it will be the first time speech has ever been communicated to an aeroplane in flight. Dip if you are hearing me.' The plane obligingly dipped.)

After the war Eckersley joined Prince at Marconi at Writtle, near Chelmsford, Essex. There he continued to research wireless equipment for aircraft. The young engineers also built a transmitter and made experimental broadcasts to amateur wireless enthusiasts. 'More and more people became interested in the possession of an apparatus which, fantastically, picked music out of the air,' he recalled.

The Writtle engineers broadcast from a hut in a field for half an hour a week on Wednesday evenings. 'We only thought of it as another job of work for which we would be blamed if it went wrong and hardly noticed if it went right,' remembered Eckersley. One evening he went out for a pub supper before coming in to broadcast. He took charge of the microphone suitably fortified. 'A certain ebullience, which often overcomes me when I have an audience, prompted a less formal attitude towards the microphone than was customary,' he remembered. 'I failed to play all the records . . . and I went on talking and talking.'

Head office was 'shocked by my frivolity' but fifty or more postcards of admiration from listeners came in. Another step in the history of broadcasting: it could be funny, it could be made delightful by a clever man larking about; it could be a carrier of wit and humour. 'It was all rather fun. Doubtless at times I was horribly facetious, but I did try to be friendly and talk with, rather than at, my listeners.' He had, quite by chance, become the first wireless comedian. He had alighted on one of the essential qualities of the radio – it was fundamentally a friendly and intimate medium.

Eckersley joined the BBC in 1923, its chief and only engineer. His first job was to build a London transmitter: he chose his spot by climbing to the roof of Marconi House on Kingsway, surveying the skyline, and then setting off to find the chimney of a distant electricity-generating station in Marylebone. Six and a half years later, he had a team of almost four hundred, and transmitters marching across the British landscape. Aside from Reith and a very few other pioneers, he was perhaps the most important figure in the early BBC: he made it work. But his views were out of joint with Reithian ideology. The idea of the BBC as a great public institution, its values enshrined as national virtues, was regarded as bunkum by Eckersley: 'Commercial broadcasting would undoubtedly have been instituted in Britain', had it not been for a shortage of wavelengths, he argued. He explained, 'When British broadcasting started the Postmaster thought that the best way to use the limited technical facilities available for broadcasting was to appoint a single agent to do all

The 1930s transmitter at Broadcasting House looms
over the spire of All Souls, Langham Place.

broadcasting in Britain. The result was that he created our
all-powerful and all-boring BBC.' The early ruling to avoid
advertising 'was only made to save trouble . . . if the number of listeners had been small, and the funds to run the
service therefore inadequate, the [BBC] would no doubt

have forgotten the sociological issue and saved itself a lot of money by getting advertisers to put on programmes … I have often thought that if there had been a world short-age of celluloid, as there is a shortage of wireless channels, we might even now be suffering the soporific of a nation-alised cinema.' Eckersley did, however, recognise the importance of a 'rich and centralised BBC' in hastening the development of the market for television, since the BBC could 'afford to test if consumer demand [was] big enough'. In the US, he argued, TV was caught in an early bind because advertisers, the funders of the programmes, were unwilling to take a risk on a small number of viewers – while at the same time 'the public would not take up "viewing" without expensive television programmes to look at'.

Instinctively, though, he disliked the BBC's monopoly. He described his old employer in terms that might have its current critics nodding in agreement. The BBC, he wrote, 'is such a feeble thing compared with what it might be. It is a great bore, dull and hackneyed and pompously self-conscious . . . issues are dodged which even a com-mercial press has no fear to expose. The BBC stands, either remote and dictatorial or pawky, oblivious of opportunity, hopeless in its timidity.' Its excessive (in his view) caution was quite different from the cheerfully demotic tone of the Writtle broadcasts: 'The BBC has become the careful mouthpiece of conformity ("there is so much to be said on both sides" that the BBC lets neither side say anything), and far from being a patron of the arts it has been merely patronising towards the artists.' He compared the BBC to medieval robber barons, 'perched in their castles above the river gorges' who 'had the power to control water-borne commerce or even prevent it. In the same way the "broadcasting authority" stands over the narrows of programme flow and can pass or refuse or select for broadcasting whatever its policy dictates'.

The strength of his views was, no doubt, fuelled by his falling out with Reith, and his subsequent adventures outside the BBC, building stations in Continental Europe to beam offshore commercial radio into the UK. But, seen through Eckersley's eyes, the BBC looks as odd as would a British Publishing Corporation, producing the bulk of the nation's books; or, as he suggested, a nationalised cinema industry. The corporation's defenders could cogently argue that whatever its inherent oddnesses, whatever the historical particularities that operated at its founding, the BBC happens to work; it has sinuously bent to accommodate the times, has proved itself time and again as the greatest cultural organisation our nation has known, has inserted itself into the very DNA of Britishness. But, none the less, Eckersley reminds us that had the delicate mechanisms of history been only minutely adjusted, British broadcasting could have looked very different; that right from the beginning, its shape and constitution were contested, even from within.

But for all the dissenters and evaders and enemies, there is no large-scale organised resistance to the BBC, no truly popular uprising against it – to the bafflement, one senses, of some on the right. John Whittingdale, the Conservative MP who at the time of writing had chaired the Culture

Select Committee for a decade, holding free-market-inflected views on the BBC, was, in another life, Thatcher's political secretary. When we met at Portcullis House, he reminisced about another, unhappier adventure with a poll tax. 'I was in Downing Street as they rampaged up and down Whitehall throwing petrol bombs and attacking policemen when they were rioting against the poll tax. And it had a means-tested element, you know. You only paid 20 per cent if you were on a very low income.' He added, seeming mildly incredulous that no petrol bombs are thrown in protest against the BBC's funding regime: 'The licence fee – it doesn't matter if you haven't got two halfpennies to rub together, you still pay £145.50.' Most of us do so uncomplainingly, even gladly. For now.

PART THREE

UNCHARTED SEAS

9

'The great globe itself'

Time was once a rough and ready thing to be marked by the movements of the sun and the vagaries of the church clock. But as the nineteenth century matured, the electrical telegraph and alarm clock became the new, efficient keepers of time, regulating the railways and awakening commuters. From 1922 these technologies were joined by a yet more powerful force: the BBC. The Greenwich time signal – the 'pips' – was devised by Reith and the then astronomer royal, Frank Watson Dyson, and first broadcast on 5 February 1924. With the soaring of wireless sales through the 1920s and 1930s, the populace became synchronised to itself as never before. Time, no longer a casual, ambling thing, fell into regimented step. As the BBC's transmitters – those pencil-sharp towers of modernist promise – gradually cast their skein of radio signals across the UK, so the land itself was transformed into a kind of timepiece.

A decade after its birth, in 1932, the BBC started to broadcast on shortwave to the empire. (The service was introduced by Reith in a manner utterly out of joint with our own era's taste for hyperbole: 'Don't expect too much in the early days. The programmes will neither be very interesting nor very good.') The sound of Big Ben striking was one of the most popular features enjoyed by British subjects overseas during the 1930s, hooking the empire's dispersed peoples into a single time frame: you might have been in the outback, but Greenwich Mean Time was what mattered. An early edition of the journal *World Radio* included a letter from a listener in Malaysia who had reset the domestic clock to GMT better to catch the BBC schedule.

The BBC thus bound nationhood and time together. It also changed the nature of space – for it banished distance. 'The crofter in the north of Scotland' and 'the agricultural labourer in the west of England' could together hear 'the king speak on some great national occasion', wrote Reith in *Broadcast Over Britain*. This sense of proximity resulted, too, in a certain ironing out of regional difference in speech. In the early debates about the BBC there was plenty written on the kind of voices suitable for broadcasting: there emerged a blandly middle-class 'standard English'. Even now, though the more genteel kinds of Scottish, Welsh, Northern Irish and West Indian accents are heard on Radio 4, one does not very often hear an announcer or presenter with a deep West Country burr, or a roundly Liverpool or Birmingham accent. Hilda Matheson wrote that it was an undeniable fact 'that standard English . . . is associated with education and good breeding, while to be without it is a definite handicap to any ambitious boy or girl'. Standard English was not just about comprehensibility, then, but also aspiration – but the sometimes rather strangulated refinement of the BBC voice could irritate. A letter to the *Daily Mail* in 1929 complained, 'Sir, a person like myself, who appreciates to the full all that the British Broadcasting Corporation has done and is doing for listeners, becomes irritated beyond endurance when announcers say "Australiar", "dramar", "Indiar", "insigniar" "idear" etc as they very frequently do. Being a Scot, I do not like "warh", "Empiah, "paht" and suchlike sounds, but I *do* detest that final "r". Stop it please. A Scot.'

There are still times when we together cleave to the BBC as a nation bound in one time frame to communal experience. During the summer of 2012, millions of us cheered for Team GB at the Olympics, via the BBC. We come together for the best of Saturday-night entertainment, for the most hotly awaited drama, for significant political or royal moments (20 million tuned into the BBC's coverage of the wedding of the Duke and Duchess of Cambridge). The BBC remains a crucial carrier of British identity: it binds us recognisably to ourselves. If nationhood consists of sets of intangibles, of common reference points and belief systems, the BBC threads us together through shared experience and memory. In a phrase that would have baffled Reith, it is perhaps also the greatest British export brand, instantly associated with the UK and admired throughout the world. Within Britain, when so many national industries and services (the National Coal Board, British Steel, British Rail, Royal Mail) have been privatised and broken up, it stands alongside the NHS and our great national museums as one of a dwindling number of institutions held in common in a civic space for the benefit of all. Director general Tony Hall put it this way: the BBC conducts 'a sense of what British creativity is and how Britain expresses itself to itself . . . We are part of what makes Britain Britain, and all the eddies and currents that make up Britain flow right through the BBC.'

But just as this ninety-year age of broadcast simultaneity is passing, or at least significantly changing its nature, in the face of the proliferation of broadcasters and the rise of the catch-up service, ideas of Britain and Britishness are coming under strain too. There are two great changes afoot to the manner in which the BBC is bound to ideas of Britishness. One has already taken place almost unremarked and undebated by the general public; the second relates to the loosening of the very ties that bind the UK together as a single entity. The first is that from 1 April 2014 the Foreign Office ceased to fund the World Service – the radio, television and online news and cultural service that the BBC provides to audiences overseas. For decades it had been an expression, albeit an editorially independent one, of British 'soft power' in often sensitive territories. Now the £245 million bill is borne by licence-fee payers. For many, the change, negotiated by former director general Mark Thompson in the face of the threat that the government should cease to meet the bill for television licences for the over-seventy-fives, seemed nothing more than an apparent administrative nicety, a way of dodging an even heavier financial burden. In fact, it raised important questions about the nature and purpose of broadcasting to overseas audiences.

The second is the debate about Scotland's nationhood, which the referendum on 18 September 2014 settled in practical terms, but hardly stilled for the long term. And, while an important event in itself, the debate also served as the most obvious example of a long-term trend in Britain (echoed by similar moves on mainland Europe):

the reassertion of national and regional identities in a post-imperial age.

In its white paper on independence, it had been the Scottish National Party's policy that in the event of a 'yes' vote, BBC Scotland should be severed from the rump of the corporation and a Scottish Broadcasting Service established. Many in Scotland had been sceptical about the notion – skeletal and short on detail as it was. But even among those who believed in retaining the union were many who argued that the BBC should examine afresh how successfully it related to the constituent parts of the UK – and whether a suppler, less monolithic notion of the corporation ought to be embraced in the face of changing notions of Britishness.

In most parts of the world – with the exception of certain countries, including China, where its shortwave transmissions are jammed and its website restricted – you will not be far from the BBC (nor, these days, from other global broadcasters such as Russia Today, Al Jazeera, CNN and China's CCTV). There is the BBC website. There are the formats, programmes and channels (such as BBC Earth, BBC Lifestyle, CBeebies) that are sold around the globe by Worldwide, the BBC's commercial arm. *Strictly Come Dancing*, or *Dancing with the Stars* as it is known elsewhere, was in late 2014 the most popular format, running in 50 overseas versions. The most exported programme in its original form was *Top Gear*, followed by *Doctor Who* and *Sherlock* (a roll call that gives pause for thought about the particular view of Britishness BBC Television offered). The BBC World News channel was available in 200 countries. And the World Service broadcast radio in 28 languages and free-to-air TV in 9 languages.

The World Service – until 1965 known in turn as the External Services and General Overseas Service – is the offspring of two distinct streams in the early BBC: its English-language Empire Service, and the slightly later foreign-language services that began in 1938. The Empire Service was an address to the white ruling class, a way of bringing to scattered listeners the sounds of home – and the imaginative tools inwardly to reconstruct its physical landscapes, too. A poem published in the *World Radio* journal of 1932 put it this way:

> . . . Fancy, thus prompted by swift-winged sound,
> Shall build you fairy pictures in the air
> Of Thames and Tweed, of mountains heather-crowned,
> Of Sussex windmills whitening in the sun,
> Fens grey with rain, green meadows, furrows dun
> And London, with the Empire's House of Prayer . . .

Or as George V rather dramatically put it in an Empire Service Christmas address, it was 'for men and women so cut off by the snows, the desert or the sea that only voices out of the air can reach them'. Despite the good intentions and efforts of some BBC executives, the traffic of sound was mostly one way – from Britain and, specifically, London, to the dominions.

Foreign-language broadcasts were a direct response to the rise of shortwave transmissions from Germany and

Italy, the fascist regimes there having quickly identified the power of the wireless as a propaganda tool. On the Italian side, Mussolini was broadcasting into the Middle East – a region thick with British interests – from Bari. In 1935, when Reith spoke to the Ullswater Parliamentary Committee, there was generalised disbelief that the German government should be subsidising propaganda broadcasting to the tune of £3 million. He told the committee, 'The sort of thing they do which would lend colour to such a figure is the turning out of the Berlin Philharmonic Orchestra in the middle of the night to play to parts of the British Empire.' Lord Ullswater replied, 'You mean they keep them sitting up?' Reith drily affirmed that this was indeed the case. The British government needed to catch up.

As war loomed, the BBC's Arabic Service was established, then Portuguese and Spanish services for Latin America, then, by the time of the Munich crisis, German, Italian and French. The purpose of these broadcasts was quite different from that of the Empire Service. According to the historian Alban Webb, for the first time the BBC was 'not making the assumption that listeners have the same view as it. It was talking to people with different, and sometimes opposing, views. It was trying to manage the perception of Britain through radio.'

The BBC was transformed by the war, in all kinds of ways: its staff doubled and its news operation ascended to new levels as listeners demanded the kind of here-and-now, on-the-ground relationship with events that could be only partially satisfied by newspapers. It also fought its own battles of the airwaves: by 1943 it was, with government funding, broadcasting in 45 languages.

Charles Rolo, a British-born, American-domiciled journalist who would go on to become literary editor of the *Atlantic*, wrote a slim volume called *Radio War* (1943). Radio, he wrote, 'has been streamlined from a crude propaganda bludgeon into the most powerful single instrument of political warfare the world has ever known. More flexible in use and infinitely stronger in emotional impact than the printed world, as a weapon of war waged psychologically radio has no equal.'

In the psychological warfare conducted by the BBC, its great weapon was the truth – which is neither as simple nor as pious as it sounds. Truth became a formidable force, skilfully deployed, difficult to combat by the enemy. Truth – of course not a monolithic thing, but elastic and flexible, capable of being moulded through selection and tone and language – was the great weapon. According to Webb, 'The truth can be self-flagellation, government-bashing, and admitting failure. But admitting failure gives you more strength, and that is what Goebbels didn't get, and that's what the BBC learns in the war. And the BBC also learns that if you keep doing that, so if there's a consistency in the way you report failure and problems, then you end up with even more credibility.' By the time decisive Allied victories such as El Alamein and Stalingrad finally came, the BBC had built up enough trust for its accounts of them to be believed.

A wartime propaganda sheet proclaimed: 'Men, women and even children risk imprisonment and death to hear broadcasts from London. They are the inhabitants of the occupied countries of Europe. They do so because they have learned that the British broadcasts tell them the truth ... FROM LONDON COMES THE VOICE OF BRITAIN ... THE VOICE OF FREEDOM.' Tangye Lean, brother of the film-maker David, who was director of External Services during the war, wrote in his book *Voices in the Darkness* (1943) of a letter published in 1942 by Goebbels, suppos-edly having been sent to him from a frontline soldier. The letter analysed 'the motives inspiring the BBC's apparent preference for the truth'. What Britain counted on was 'the slogan already spread abroad before the war, and unfor-tunately one which had become a fixed conception about the decency and "fair play" of the English'. The notorious truthfulness of the BBC had morphed almost into a national characteristic – or at least a piece of useful national mythology. The 'truth' notion played into a centuries-long rhetoric of British exceptionalism: British liberty, British fair play, British imperial virtues.

In her novel *Human Voices*, Penelope Fitzgerald put it like this: 'Broadcasting House was in fact dedicated to the strangest project of the war, or of any war, that is, telling the truth. Without prompting, the BBC had decided that the truth was more important than consolation, and, in the long run, would be more effective.' The BBC, she wrote, was 'scattering human voices into the darkness of Europe'. Fitzgerald was too sly a novelist to write without ambiguity. Human voices are just that: human, and there-fore fallible. She compared the truthfulness of the BBC to that of the Delphic Oracle – notorious for locking the truth inside slanted speech, for tricking the unwary with riddles.

Towards the end of the war, much soul-searching occurred at the BBC about the future of its overseas broadcasting. Even before the onset of the cold war, the government was already recognising the value of continuing directly to fund it in what was likely to be a scenario of post-war 'disturbance'. The BBC, on the other hand, was anxious about the danger of political interference in its broadcasting agenda, unprotected as it was by the added distance from the state provided by the licence fee. From the end of the war until Foreign Office funding for the World Service ceased in the spring of 2014, there was a continuing negotiation between the BBC's 'notions of editorial integrity and independence on the one hand, and the desire to exert influence over programme-making to bring it in line with British geopolitical interests, on the other', in the words of Webb in *London Calling*, his history of the World Service during the cold war. Sir John Tusa, managing director of the World Service from 1986 to 1993, described his relationship with the Foreign Office as 'a rather sophisticated quadrille: they knew perfectly well that if they were ever seen to be directing or shaping World Service output it would undermine the whole basis of its credibility and authority worldwide'.

What of the World Service now? I spoke to Peter Horrocks not long before he stepped down as its head in 2015. He envisioned a modern service that was more about exchange and reciprocity than the old metropolitan idea of wisdom radiating into the world from Bush House.

Increasingly, locally based, bilingual journalists were bringing fresh insight to stories for the World Service, he said, and they were in turn enriching the BBC's foreign news operation as a whole – Kenyan Anne Soy, for example, who reported on the Westgate shopping mall shootings in Nairobi in 2013; or Nomsa Maseko, a South African journalist who, on the day Nelson Mandela died, movingly recalled her own memories of when he was set free. This approach in turn, Horrocks told me, might be seen as reflecting a modern sense of Britishness: one that is multicultural; one that is more porously open to world influence; one that looks a little more like what one might actually see in the streets of that world city, London.

But there remained many questions. Why should the British citizenry pay for this soft diplomacy through their licence fee? What was in it for them when the BBC supports Hausa or Somali or Kirundi services? The services in turn were placed in a position where they would have to fight their corner against domestic output rather than being protected by a separate funding structure (though the BBC would still need a Foreign Office sign-off to wholly cut, or indeed introduce, a language service). Would the World Service end up being simply absorbed into the foreign news operation, with no identity or role of its own? At the same time, moves to support the World Service commercially were also causing disquiet, on two fronts – first, that the BBC's enormous brand power could attract advertising revenues away from less mighty competitors; second, that the enduring reputation of the World

Service for accurate, even-handed news coverage could be undermined by the intrusion of commercial concerns.

Allan Little had been a BBC foreign correspondent in many countries. When we met, in a cafe in Edinburgh in the spring of 2014, he told me about reporting from Freetown during the Sierra Leonian civil war, seeing the whole of Siaka Stevens Street stop dead as people crowded 'in every doorway, on every market stall' round transistors to hear the World Service's *Focus on Africa*. He remembered the elderly Jewish man in Paris who agreed to give him an interview because as a boy in hiding in wartime Poland the BBC was the only way he knew to keep on hoping; he remembered the old independence fighter in Zimbabwe who 'hated the British' yet 'in secret, when he wanted to know what was happening in the world, he said, "We listened to you and we trusted you."' Little regarded the trust placed in the World Service and the BBC, fiercely guarded across the world and over generations, as a kind of covenant. 'What a legacy. What an inheritance,' he said. 'I worry that this is not understood in Britain by the licence-fee payer who just reads how crap the BBC is every day in the papers. I worry especially now that the World Service is funded by the licence fee and has to take its chances alongside the ballgowns of *Strictly Come Dancing* and the special effects in *Doctor Who*.'

When we spoke, Little was in the thick of reporting the run-up to the Scottish referendum on independence. The months before the vote had seen the BBC occupy a delicate position. Its own institutional fate was intimately bound up with the fate of the union. And, unlike any other organisation that stood to be divided in the case of a yes vote, it was also charged with reflecting and reporting the referendum campaigns impartially. The BBC had reacted to that problem by declining to comment on or discuss any potential break-up of the corporation, even in private – there was no paper trail inside the organisation that could have been subject to a freedom-of-information request. And yet there must have been internal conversations, scenario-planning quietly taking place off the books.

There were some in Scotland who believed that the BBC's very nature, as a pan-British broadcaster, hampered its attempts to report fairly the events that could lead to its own transformation; as a British broadcaster, it must inevitably have a pro-union bias. Many felt that the vivid and urgent debate on Scottish nationhood had been under-represented by the BBC, certainly in its main UK coverage, until the months immediately preceding the vote. For others, objections to the nature of the coverage lay in the observation that knowledge of the Scottish situation varied wildly between individual journalists. There were those within the BBC in Scotland who complained of a lack of understanding from colleagues in London: a certain failure of imagination in grasping the emotions and arguments of the Yes campaign, even a sneer creeping into the voice when the Yes camp was discussed. As the referendum approached, disquiet about the BBC's coverage increased to the point where protests were held outside its Glasgow headquarters, with the BBC's political editor, Nick Robinson, marked out for special ire from elements of the Yes camp, who saw his reporting as unbalanced. For some, the BBC became a metonym of the argument as a whole. Just as to many in Scotland it seemed objectionable that decisions about Scotland should be taken in Westminster, so it seemed objectionable that decisions about Scottish broadcasting should be taken in Portland Place.

The relationship between the BBC and the UK at large has never been uncontested or straightforward. Of Scottish audiences, only 48 per cent, according to the corporation's 2012–13 annual report, believed that the BBC was good at representing the life of their nation (as opposed to 50 per cent of Northern Irish, 53 per cent of Welsh and 58 per cent of English audiences). Since 1922 the BBC has had an especially careful path to tread in Northern Ireland. David Elstein compared the great buildings established by the BBC outside London – the new MediaCity HQ in Salford; Pacific Quay, the David Chipperfield glass-and-sandstone box on the Clyde in Glasgow – to the castles thrown up by Edward I in Wales.

Be they imperial fortresses or not, they are also projections of certain specific kinds of modernity – prefigured by John Birt's last speech as director general, in which he urged, 'We need to dismantle the dingy, cramped mid-twentieth-century warrens we currently inhabit, and to create modern, open, technically advanced workplaces' – as if only certain kinds of architectural carapace could contain and project the digital future he glimpsed on the horizon. Peter Salmon, head of BBC North, told me that he had visited California tech companies to seek inspiration for the Salford building: 'We wanted the place to be very obviously a BBC building, you know, full of BBC values but to feel like it was a younger media company with the colour schemes and the collaboration areas and the kitchens, and the use of space, and the use of technology.' Salmon was dazzled by the Google offices, but those of Pixar were those he felt most drawn to: 'I loved the feel, I loved the way it felt non-hierarchical. I loved the sense of creatives as heroes, as it were, with a creative mission that everybody seemed to share.'

The Pacific Quay building in Glasgow is a simple design with sandstone-built studios stacked in the centre of a vast top-lit box edged with offices. The feeling, when I visited in May 2014, was calm and austere. Reith's imposing, eighteenth-century clawfoot desk struck a curious note, a grand old object stranded amid the defiantly new, its leather-covered surface indented with the stains left by the first DG's tea cups. It stood near the workstation of Ken MacQuarrie, the controller of BBC Scotland – who would sit there, he said jokingly, when he wanted to feel 'particularly Reithian'. From the window I spotted the square towers of the church where Reith's father preached. In the foreground was the imposing Finnieston crane, once used for loading locomotives on to ships for export, now retained as a symbol of the Clyde's heritage.

The BBC was the new industry for this patch of Glasgow. But, rising up four square and imposing from the riverbank, it looked a little lonely, a great vessel stranded. Despite the new hotel that was being thrown up alongside it when I visited (soon, I was sure, to be filled with visiting BBC staff), despite the scattering of digital businesses around it, the economic downturn had put paid, at least for a time, to the bustling townscape that was supposed to have accompanied it: a street of shops and restaurants was to have been constructed, stretching from the BBC offices to the nearest subway station. The BBC buildings at Salford and at Pacific Quay had been conceived not simply as broadcasting offices and studios but tools of post-industrial urban regeneration.

The early BBC contains a story of the waxing and waning of the power of its non-metropolitan stations. In the 1920s local and relay stations – in places such as Stoke, Hull and Nottingham – broadcast their own services, a distant precursor to the BBC local-radio networks established in the late 1960s. But as the building of high-power transmitters enabled London to broadcast nationally, the local services were swept up into larger, tidier regional schemes, providing listeners with an 'alternative programme' to that on the national service. The essential move, according to Asa Briggs's history of the BBC, was towards metropolitanism: 'The BBC was following all the other mass media of the early twentieth century in bolstering London's supremacy, and the proud "provincialism" of the Victorian age, already in tatters in many parts of the country, continued to fade unlamented until long after the Second World War.' There were rearguard actions: reporting on conditions in the regional services in 1936, Charles Siepmann, Hilda Matheson's successor as head of talks, urged against over-centralisation, noting that 'the provinces are the seed ground of talent'.

Siepmann was thinking of broadcasters such as Olive Shapley, who had started work for the Manchester station in 1935. (On her first day she said to a female colleague, 'I know nothing about broadcasting; you must help me.' The reply came: 'The first thing you have to know, dear, is how the gentlemen take their tea.') Two years later, she was given access to one of the first mobile broadcasting units, a 27-foot truck that toddled along at a maximum speed of 20 mph. Her first programme made on the road was called *£sd: A Study in Shopping*. 'We caused a sensation when we parked the thing in Sowerby Bridge. I, feeling an utter fool and holding a microphone at the end of a long lead . . . recorded a conversation between a shop assistant and a millworker . . . In a humble way, I think we were making broadcasting history,' she recalled in her memoir. 'For a year or two I lived a strange life, in the cabs of long-distance lorries, down coalmines, in dosshouses, on long-boats on the canals . . . nothing could stop me.'

But her efforts to describe the warp and weft of northern life were not always well received. In 1939 she made a series called *Canal Journey*, interviewing men and women working on the Leeds–Liverpool waterway. She recalled that the *Listener* radio critic complained of 'obscure dialect' that was 'downright unintelligible'; the writer was 'prepared to swear that very few Londoners understood more than one word in six'. Shapley remembered thinking, 'So much for bringing the voice of the people to the nation!'

The theory of the regional stations, according to Peter Eckersley, was that each should be 'typical of the taste and culture of the region it served . . . [The scheme] gave full scope for enthusiastic and non-conforming programme directors to use their new wavelength experimentally.' Eckersley strongly deprecated what happened in practice: he felt that they had been unable to liberate themselves from the stranglehold of Broadcasting House, and the scheme was 'used as an overflow of accumulated "hotchpotch" material rather than an outlet for new ideas'. (This was perhaps somewhat unfair, given the work of Shapley and others; there comes to mind, for example, W. H. Auden's play *On Hadrian's Wall*, with a score by Benjamin Britten, broadcast from Newcastle in 1937.) As so often an anti-establishment voice within the BBC, Eckersley reached the conclusion that a true 'alternative programme' would be provided only if the regional stations were cut free and funded commercially.

But as Eckersley himself pointed out, commercial broadcasting was already a going concern in Britain by 1929, 'if not illegal . . . [then] frowned upon by grandmotherly authority . . . Wireless waves flip across frontiers with persistent disregard for regulation,' he wrote. Stations such as Radio Normandie sprang up, based on the Continent but broadcasting into Britain. Their success, he drily noted, was aided by Reith's strong sabbatarianism: Sunday programming at the BBC was limited in quantity and dull in quality. 'The ordinary listener did not feel that he was committing any sin in being amused on Sunday and turned from what he considered dreary local broadcasting to amusing foreign programmes,' he wrote.

Radios Normandie and Luxembourg were the ancestors of the buccaneering offshore 'pirate' stations such as Caroline and London – training grounds of figures such as Kenny Everett, Dave Lee Travis and John Peel, in the early 1960s providing the musical education of many a young listener for whom the BBC's Light Programme was an irrelevance. In 1967 the pirates were effectively outlawed by the Marine Broadcasting Offences Act, and Radio 1 created as a nationalised pop station employing many of the former offshore DJs.

That same year, and as a result of the recommendations of the Pilkington Committee on Broadcasting of 1962, BBC local radio was also established. It was intended, wrote Frank Gillard, then the corporation's director of sound broadcasting, as 'a running serial story of local life in all its aspects . . . the relationship between local radio station and local paper would not be one of competition' (a claim that has long been disputed, especially in the current era of depletion of the local press). The third local station to start broadcasting, on 14 March 1968, was Radio Stoke. One of the voices first heard was that of John Snagge, who had broadcast for the 1920s relay station 6ST, Radio Stoke's ancestor. He began: 'This is BBC Radio Stoke-on-Trent. We must apologise to listeners for the break in transmission which occurred at twelve o'clock midnight, on October 30th, 1928. This was due to circumstances beyond our control. Normal transmission has now been resumed.'

Radio Stoke was four years old when I was born, and it broadcast into the neighbourhood where I grew up. I spent a day in the station in the spring of 2014. In the years that separated that visit from my childhood, Stoke had transformed completely: when I was young it was a landscape of pottery factories and mines, but, though some manufacturing remained, it was much diminished. But Radio Stoke was still there, vying for listeners with the local independent station, Signal. In the 10.10 a.m. news meeting (only one woman present), the stories were of the potential impact of the high-speed rail link HS2; of the possibility of fracking in the county; and of the extraction of methane gas (the last a remnant of the long-gone mining industry). A hugely important, long-running story had concerned the poor care and high mortality rate at Stafford Hospital in the south of the county, which had led to a public inquiry and the dissolution of the trust that ran it. Someone talked about the compulsory purchase of a city-centre pub for development; another of cars parked on pavements, causing problems for disabled people and those with young children.

Later, I spoke to Ajmal Hussain, who presented a show on the station: he told me about trying to present a nuanced picture of the sizeable local Asian community. 'They just really want an honest view of themselves without the conversation automatically turning to grooming, to forced marriages, to terrorism, which is where it tends to go to,' he said. Terry Goodwin, the station's news editor, spoke to me of the importance of reflecting back to itself 'a place that it doesn't feel like it's very well loved from the outside. That's the thing that Radio Stoke does: it really cares about the city and it cares about the area, which, let's be honest, a lot of the country doesn't.'

*

In Scotland, I had found that one did not have to talk to many people about the BBC before hearing a note of exasperation. There was clearly a great deal of passionate love for the BBC – enough for the Scottish National Party's white paper on independence to have felt the need to reassure voters that 'programmes like *EastEnders*, *Doctor Who*, and *Strictly Come Dancing*, and channels like CBeebies will still be available in Scotland'. But people both within and beyond the BBC spoke to me – off the record, in the sensitive period running up to the referendum – of decades-long frustration, despite a number of concerted efforts by the BBC to improve, in its news coverage, its feeling for national difference. Scots told me of waking up to headlines on nurses' pay – except in Scotland it was different. Of teachers strikes 'across the country' – except in Scotland it was different. Of legal matters, of the NHS, of cigarette packaging, of school examination results, of local elections. Except in Scotland it was different. The inverse was also true: serious events in Scotland were, it was felt, under-represented on the national bulletins.

As far back as 1944, a pamphlet, published in the run-up to a charter renewal by the Saltire Society, urged that 'revenue from Scottish licence fees' should be 'spent in Scotland', and demanded the development of an 'enlightened and stimulating Scottish Broadcasting Service . . . What we have aimed at is best described, perhaps, as a Broadcasting Service with frequent international contacts, initiated from Scotland and designed to meet the needs and wishes of Scottish listeners.' Not a million miles away from what was being proposed by the Yes campaign in 2014.

A sense of dislocation between Scottish listeners and the BBC was only increased when the nation gained a devolved parliament in 1998. With colleagues, the then head of BBC Scotland, John McCormick, devised the notion of a Scottish six o'clock TV news bulletin. It would run for an hour, replacing the regional bulletin, *Reporting Scotland*, which started at 6.30 p.m. In Queen Margaret Drive, the old Glasgow HQ, it didn't feel like an especially radical move: after all, the nation had its own news bulletins on BBC Radio Scotland. And there would be a fresh news agenda provided by Holyrood. There would be some tweaks to the running order and a consolidation of news concerning Scotland. Viewers had found it irritatingly repetitive, for example, when a Scottish story that had been low down the running order in the British bulletin was the lead five minutes later on *Reporting Scotland*. The notion was to keep the 1 p.m. and 9 p.m. programmes untouched: the 6 p.m. had always been weighted towards domestic news.

The Broadcasting Council for Scotland, which provided audience feedback from the nation to the governors, and the impeccably establishment Norman Drummond, a Church of Scotland minister and the BBC governor for Scotland, were strongly in favour of the idea. The governors as a whole were divided, with the chair, Sir Christopher Bland, keeping his cards close to his chest. The director Sir Richard Eyre, then a governor, was pro. He recalled, '[The DG] John Birt's thesis was that the BBC was a crucial binding agent in making Great Britain great. My view – I'd lived in Scotland for six years – was that it was the opposite. I think it's incredibly divisive and you only have to spend a bit of time in Scotland to realise that the BBC is regarded as English broadcasting and those feelings run very, very deep. I said you could achieve a very clever piece of politics by enfranchising a Scottish news at six.'

Birt was utterly opposed to the Scottish Six. In *The Harder Path*, he described the episode as 'a bitter battle to prevent the BBC being split apart by the fissiparous forces of devolution'. The Scottish Six risked the unity of the BBC, and in turn of Britain itself. The Six would be the thin end of the wedge:

> I was deeply resistant to the proposal. It could have dire consequences for the BBC and unintended consequences for the United Kingdom . . . once the Six was conceded there would be no argument for resisting the takeover of the One and the Nine as well. Within a few years there would be no UK-wide news on the BBC. I calculated that this domino effect would continue, with a momentum of its own, until eventually the BBC itself was either turned into a weak, federal institution – each part going its own way – or was broken up, with an English Broadcasting Corporation headquartered in London.

Talking to a BBC employee who had been connected with the process at the time, it was clear how frustrating this reasoning had been: Birt, with his perhaps rather literal turn of mind, was convinced that the other bulletins would follow the Six into Scottish oblivion – but, I was told, just because there was a certain logic to his prediction, did not mean that it would actually happen, or that anyone particularly wanted it to happen.

Arguments were spat forth over October and November 1998. There was horror when a document on news strategy was published – with no mention of a potential Scottish Six – before the governors had taken their decision. It looked like a stitch-up, a fait accompli. The splash in the *Daily Record* for 26 November 1998 read: 'Wanted: for the cold-blooded murder of Scotland's own news programme.' There were mugshots of the BBC executives concerned – including that of Tony Hall, now the director general, then the head of news.

Only later, courtesy of his memoir, did it emerge that Birt had made a direct approach to the prime minister, Tony Blair, to keep the powerful cohort of Scottish Labour MPs on side. A Scottish Six would 'encourage separatist tendencies', Birt argued. Blair agreed, and asked Peter Mandelson to marshal Labour's forces; later James Purnell, then an adviser at Number 10, who later returned to the BBC as director of strategy and digital, took on the task. A decade and a half later, Birt's appeal to the government still hurt and bewildered those who were involved in the Scottish Six plans – BBC loyalists whose intention was not to threaten the institution but to improve its service for its audience.

Bland, at the time pleading compromise, sounded implacable on the argument when I spoke to him before the

Scottish referendum, in early 2014. 'The idea that there's a Scottish view of the war in Kosovo or the Afghanistan war is just nonsense,' he said. 'It would be hugely expensive, totally pointless and just satisfying a foolish wish for a tartan-badged news.' The ideas for an SBS were fanciful, he thought. 'If there were genuinely to be a Scottish Broadcasting Corporation with a Scottish licence fee and Scottish audience, it would be strapped for cash and talent. The Scots benefit, as do the Welsh and the Northern Irish, as do we all, from a unified and strong organisation because of the importance of scale. You can't afford four separate newsrooms. You just can't.' Birt also entered the fray before the referendum: writing for the *Guardian*, he warned of a Yes vote resulting in a diminished BBC for the rump of the UK and a small, enfeebled Scottish Broadcasting Service. Scottish viewers would end up having to pay to see BBC programmes, whether by subscribing to channels or by the SBS's buying in shows. 'Whatever is asserted wishfully in the white paper, the BBC will have no alternative but to act in the interests of its licence payers and to seek the best possible commercial terms for the sale of its programmes in Scotland, not least because of the financial impoverishment it will just have suffered. And, of course, there may be commercial broadcasters in a new Scotland willing to pay more for the BBC's most successful programmes than an impecunious SBS,' he wrote. It was all about scale, he argued: a Yes vote would result in Scots being unable to enjoy the possibility, open to them since the 1707–8 Act of Union, of making a 'massive impact on a big stage'.

Needless to say, that was not the view of those behind the SNP's white paper on the future of Scotland. The SNP's vision was of a Scottish Broadcasting Service built on Scotland's share of the licence fee and a proportionate share of BBC Worldwide profits. Viewers would be better off than they had been hitherto because, according to the SNP's figures, they would have twice the income as the sum currently spent by the BBC in Scotland (£345 million a year as opposed to £175 million). Under a proposed joint venture with the BBC, Scottish audiences would continue to receive BBC channels and services in exchange for programming created in Scotland. The SBS would also create a new TV channel and radio network. The SNP was looking towards Germany, with its federalised, regional broadcasters; and Denmark, with its successful recent stint of international drama hits, with enthusiasm.

This negotiating position hung in the air: there was no sign that the BBC accepted the SNP's figures, or would be willing to embark on a joint venture, or would regard Scottish productions such as *River City* and *Shetland* as a fair 'swap' for *EastEnders* and *Strictly Come Dancing*. Notions of precisely how a new national broadcaster would be constituted were only lightly sketched in. Independence from government, regulation and governance were unclear: there was no detailed blueprint. Meanwhile, staff at BBC Scotland were nervously awaiting their fates. The white paper stated that the SBS would be 'initially' founded on the staff and assets of BBC Scotland.

On 18 September the voters decided, by a margin of 55 to 45 per cent, to remain in the Union – and, by extension, to continue their relationship with the BBC. But, like the UK as a whole, the corporation still had choices to make in the wake of the existential debates that renewed and animated political discourse in Scotland. How the BBC responds in the long term is crucial – not just for the population of Scotland, but for everyone in the UK. Its actions will go beyond narrow questions of broadcasting policy and into the realms of nationhood and identity, of which the BBC is such a profoundly important carrier. In the future, the BBC will have to demonstrate that it can express multiple and interlocking identities through all parts of the UK with suppleness, sensitivity and understanding.

10

'The monoliths will shake'

'There were no sealed orders to open. The commission was of the scantiest nature. Very few knew what broadcasting meant; none knew what it might become.' So John Reith in 1924 recalled the previous eighteen months of his life as the general manager of the brand-new British Broadcasting Company. What Reith did recognise, instinctively and immediately, was the magnitude of his responsibility: 'There was something big, even colossal, conveyed in the nature of the contract which had been undertaken.' Reith and his 'bohemian flock' (as head of variety Eric Maschwitz described the band of early colleagues) were out to invent the future. Reith, that monstrous, tyrannical, tortured man, set his furious gaze at the new technological world of wireless telegraphy and saw that it could be, should be, placed in the service of society as a whole. The job was to 'establish a certain number of broadcasting stations and transmit therefrom, at certain times, programmes composed of whatever a programme can be composed', he wrote, but he knew that was only the most mechanistic and banal way of describing the task and the opportunity. What Reith saw was that he had in his hands an instrument that could inform, educate and entertain not just the privileged – but everyone.

In 1922, only a handful of wireless pioneers actually owned sets (we might think of them as like the Internet enthusiasts of the early 1990s, eccentric outriders in whose footsteps few realised we were all to follow). Peter Eckersley had yet to stud the landscape with the transmitters that would allow a BBC service to fan out to all parts of the UK. And yet Reith saw that broadcasting could one day have a number of extraordinary qualities. First, that the licence fee – often now characterised as an unpleasant piece of regressive taxation – was in fact a passport to equality. No one would be able to pay more and get a better BBC; there would be no first, second or third class. 'The same music rings as sweetly in mansion as in cottage . . . There is nothing in it which is exclusive to those who pay more, or who are considered in one way or another more worthy of attention.' So wrote Reith in *Broadcast Over Britain*.

Second, everyone would be able to access the BBC in private. Your tastes, your culture, your enthusiasms, your politics – all of these could be developed without the eye of anyone upon you. If you closed the door, no one, not the busybodies down the road, nor the religious authorities, nor the government could track what you were listening to. (It is no coincidence that, during the Third Reich, communal television viewing in *Fernsehstuben*, public 'television parlours' was encouraged: private tastes and ideas are dangerous to a certain kind of regime.) 'An event, be it speech, or music, or play, or ceremony is certainly broadcast for any and all to receive, but it seems to be personal to the individual hearer, and is brought to his very room,' wrote Reith of the simultaneously public and private quality of broadcasting.

Third, Reith was convinced that broadcasting, with this peculiar capability of reaching everyone, should also provide for everyone. Using the privilege brought by the income from the licence fee, it should serve the thinly scattered few as well as the many. 'With us, "minorities" are very important sections of the community, and a "limited appeal" may still involve many hundreds of thousands,' he wrote.

In the 1920s, the BBC had no past, only a future. It had plenty of difficulties to negotiate – then as now, a hostile and protective press, a government to convince of its ideas, enormous practical and technical hurdles. But compared with the present time, when the BBC is both beloved institution and political and cultural battle ground, an organisation whose every movement is minutely examined and raked over, it was free: a start-up with an inventive young team, idealistic and experimental. Maschwitz recalled the company's first headquarters: 'Savoy Hill was like a small, excited club whose members came in to work in the early morning and stayed on until Big Ben chimed midnight – for the good reason that there was always something interesting afoot.' The first chapter of *Broadcast Over Britain* is called 'Uncharted Seas', and that was what there was: a vast and empty ocean of possibility. The first BBC director of programmes, Arthur Burrows, in *The Story of Broadcasting*, also published in 1924, used the same metaphor: 'What lies ahead in that uncharted sea, the future? Broadcasting today, despite its appeal to the public imagination, is really only in the position of the prehistoric fisherman who put out a few hundred yards from shore in his frail coracle or dug-out . . . We may be certain, therefore, that the work of the past few years . . . is but shallow-water fishing in relation to ocean navigation.' In those early days, it had the rickety sense of possibility and excitement that we might associate with a start-up today. Cecil Lewis was already nostalgic by 1924:

> Great days! Already I look back on them with a certain wistfulness and regret . . . The microphone that is tied up with bits of string, the switches that are falling to pieces, and the gadgets that won't work unless they are coaxed by someone who knows how. When things don't always work infallibly! When something goes wrong and one has to step into the breach and talk nonsense for half an hour . . . isn't it preferable, after all, to the watertight compartments and petty differences that come later in the well-built organisations? . . . It was a democracy – short-lived alas! A democracy of young pioneers . . . doomed to be swept quickly into the inexorable mills of civilisation and organisation.

There is a quality of inventiveness, ingenuity and resourcefulness that has run through the BBC. That no engineer, digital or otherwise, now sits on the executive board, would have surprised Peter Eckersley – for him the BBC was as importantly an engineering company as a broadcaster, and he and his successors had the institutional clout to match. He himself foresaw multichannel cable TV (as well as air-conditioning and double-glazing) in 1941. 'I have a dream about the future. I see the interior of a living room. The wide windows are formed from double panes of glass, fixed and immovable. The conditioned air is fresh and warm . . . flush against the wall there is a translucent screen with numbered strips of lettering running across it . . . These are the titles describing the many different "broadcasting" programmes which can be heard by just pressing the corresponding button,' he wrote.

John Birt had a similar moment of vatic clarity, albeit over a shorter time frame, in his last speech as director general, in 1999. In years to come, he said:

> You will carry with you wherever you go a mobile device to gain instant access to the many bounties of this world . . . it will enable us to call up programmes and services on demand, at a moment of our choosing . . . anyone will be able to make and to publish their own programmes . . . In a total digital world, no one will wait about for a programme of their choice to be transmitted. They will want all programmes on demand at a time of their choosing. They will want services that focus on their personal passions, perspectives and needs. And they will want those services to be available on all media, wherever they are – at home; in the workplace; or on the move.

It was a pretty accurate piece of prophecy bearing in mind that he was speaking six years before YouTube was activated in February 2005, and eight years before the release of the iPhone in June 2007 and the launch of iPlayer that December. In fact iPlayer was the product, so BBC folk memory goes, of a drunken night out in 2003 after a digital worker got into trouble posting an inappropriate photograph of the model Katie Price on the BBC Three website. Requiring a redemptive idea to stave off disgrace, he and colleagues came up with the notion of a video-on-demand service for the channel. Four years and 86 internal meetings later, iPlayer was born. Such is the frequently unheroic nature of invention.

What are the ideas that will sustain the BBC in the years to come? Birt's vision of services customised for individuals is yet to be fully realised – but when we met, Tony Hall, the director general, told me it would be just round the corner. The BBC, as accessed through the web, would soon understand and reflect your innermost desires and delights, and will offer you more and more, across all its genres, based on your past preferences. Importantly, it would do this disinterestedly: it would not try to sell you other services, or pass on details of your private predilections to any third party. It was an intriguing conceptual change, since the BBC has always, hitherto, speculatively dangled offerings at us based not on the past, the history of our preferences, but rather on a sense of the sheer largeness and variety of the world: that was the old trick of the 'hammock', whereby a skilled scheduler might sneak an unlikely but intriguing programme into the evening's line-up between two hits, and offer viewers something that no algorithm could ever predict.

The BBC would also connect you to others who share those interests, according to Hall, and would build communities of viewers digitally. We were talking in summer

2014, on the day of one of his weekly visits to programme-makers, near the set of *EastEnders* – that oddly unscruffy patch of London lovingly made at the BBC's studios in Elstree, in Hertfordshire. 'It goes back to the licence-fee payers being our owners. There's a community around *Springwatch* of over 400,000 people and they are know-ledgeable, and they care, and they're passionate,' he explained, by way of example. The BBC had had a long history of interactivity with its audiences, from the already hefty postbag of the 1920s and 1930s, to the letters pages of the *Radio Times*, vivid from the start, through to the message boards and blogs of the late twentieth and early twenty-first centuries. But, arguably, it had never quite settled on a consistent digital platform to suit its audiences, and some online communities – such as the Radio 3 and *Archers* message boards, whose contributors were often deeply critical of BBC policy – have been closed down by the BBC. In 2014, if you wanted to talk with others about programmes such as *The Great British Bake-off* or *The Archers*, Twitter was already established as the place to do it, along with popular live blogs. But the BBC was now tackling the notion of community with fresh vigour, ready to open a channel for direct, unmediated communication with audiences.

The BBC had traditionally been something of a fortress; you have been either within it or outside. Hall told me he was determined to change that. The corporation must and would become 'porous', he said. Instead of the portcullis being shut the BBC would, in the future, send its audiences out of the castle precincts and towards the work of other organisations whose values it shares. 'We should be a gateway to other people who think like us, to other people who are funded like us, to other people who have the same mission as us,' he said. 'I hope, for example, that eventually, if you want to know about Shakespeare, we will give you our content, and we will give you content from the Royal Shakespeare Company. Why wouldn't we act as a curator and send you to places that we think have good-quality content?'

The BBC would, he said, share its resources and work with organisations outside, too: 'If you're paid for by everybody it's your job to be porous. That doesn't mean you lower standards – no, no, no. You are elitist about your standards but you should be porous in terms of the people that you're inviting in to share our space.' But there were already concerns within the cultural world that the BBC's vision of artistic organisations worth working with was narrow, and that working with the BBC was, in the words of one curator, 'an absolute nightmare . . . They turn up mob-handed and they want to own everything.' When I put this to Hall he simply nodded. 'I've said it myself.' When he worked at the Royal Opera House, he used to long for the BBC to 'make their minds up and take a decision'. So how could that change? 'I want managers – and this is a change in culture – I want managers to feel valued. I think we've dumped on managers in the BBC and in our culture broadly, and not seen what I think is really important, which is that management is an art, management is about enabling, management is about giving confidence, management is about ensuring people are doing the very best work of their lives. That's what managers are there to do.'

Hall's BBC, he said, needed to give people 'the ability to fail'. Part of the idea behind the BBC's proposal, in 2014, to migrate the channel BBC Three online was to allow formats and programmes to loosen up and become more web-friendly: giving chances, for example, for comics to test out short chunks of material in a low-stakes way. What had struck him, he said, about Silicon Valley was 'the sense that we're going to try ideas – and if they don't work, we'll go somewhere else. I urge people in the BBC to do this: I say, "You will have failures, and if you are going to fail, fail fast, but don't be embarrassed about it."' He added, 'We must be the risk capital for the UK. We have got to be the people who have enough confidence to be able to say that we are going to back things that may not work. The national discourse is difficult on failure, but actually, we should be bold enough to say, "That didn't work, but good luck to those people who tried, and now let's move on and try something else."'

This rhetoric of a porous BBC hinted at a profound change in the corporation's status. Twenty years ago, the BBC stood high and proud, dear for her reputation through the world. Her dominance – notwithstanding, of course, competition with ITV and, later, Channel 4 – was uncontested. But what about a BBC that is operating on the web: a global, commercialised space that is minimally regulated, dominated by the economic models of the west coast of the US, and formally organised so as to enable the circulation and sharing of material in unprecedented ways?

The BBC's research and development department in west London contained an area known as the Blue Room, a space in which the latest tech and gadgets were laid out ready for curious employees to discover. Here, for example, demonstrators showed me an Oculus Rift: an item of snorkel-like headgear enabling one to experience a 360-degree virtual-reality space. It was financed originally on Kickstarter, was bought by Facebook, and when I visited in 2014 had not quite reached the open market. I placed the equipment on my head and suddenly I was 'in' a Tuscan villa, rendered in detailed if slightly clunky computer-game-style graphics. I wandered jerkily through it, out into its walled garden with cypress trees, and the view of the hills beyond. It made me nauseous all afternoon. But it was also clearly a thing of immense, if somewhat uncanny, possibility – and not just for gaming, perhaps its most obvious application. The BBC had already been experimenting with filming musicians from the BBC Philharmonic in 360 degrees: imagine being able to 'walk among' the musicians, hearing the balance of the music change as you move. Ralph Rivera, the director of BBC future media, had joked to me about the BBC's building a holodeck – the virtual-reality space that, in *Star Trek*, Starfleet personnel enter for recreation (or, perhaps more accurately, to explore the ontological problems posed by the scriptwriters). But it wasn't quite a joke: this is what he meant – a future in which storytelling could be made absolutely enveloping and deeply immersive.

The Blue Room also contained examples of lightfield cameras, which allow photographs to be refocused and perspective changed, creating what might be thought of as a 3D image. Matthew Postgate, controller of R&D, gave me an example of the kind of early thinking the BBC is doing with such technologies:

> We had an experiment in which we filmed a basketball match in one of our research studios. It was filmed by cameras from different angles, and had microphones all around it. We changed that into a software model, so we took that bit of video and essentially made it into the kind of environment that you'd find in a computer game, and because it's in software you can choose any camera angle you want and in real time. Equally, because it's in software, conceivably you could be incorporating that with a game and be 'playing' alongside those players.

These were visions of a future BBC in which storytelling might exit the flat surface of the screen and embrace and envelop the audience – an audience that might be increasingly active in moulding the story itself. But the Blue Room also contained something of perhaps more immediate concern to the corporation. One section of it was arranged so as to resemble a teenager's bedroom – bunk beds, football posters, the usual detritus. A real fourteen-year-old's activities on his computer were tracked after he came in from school one night, and visitors could watch the way he used his screen – he mucked around on Facebook, watched football highlights on YouTube, Skyped his friends, did a spot of homework using Wikipedia. He did not at any point access BBC material. According to figures assembled by the BBC in 2014, sixteen- to twenty-four-year-olds consumed less television (ITV and Channel 4, too) than their older counterparts. BBC1, for example, had a reach of 59.2 per cent in this age group, as opposed to 77.6 per cent for the general population (these figures related to watching on television; they did not include viewing on computers, tablets or phones). Whether this was a matter of real concern was moot – BBC research also showed that this age group had always consumed much less television than the general population; and in fact in 2014 eighteen-year-olds were consuming a shade more TV (again, on an actual set – data-gathering was lagging behind new modes of viewing) than those aged twenty-three or twenty-eight. Radio 1, directly out to serve a youth audience, had seen its listenership rise over the past decade, its controller Ben Cooper told me – from under 9.5 million in 2003 to 10.5 million. But, he added, listeners spent significantly less time with the material: 6 hours 34 minutes a week, rather than 10 hours a week in 2006.

The habits of these digital natives raised questions for the BBC, as they did for all broadcasters. Were those young people harbingers of a future in which linear television eventually, in some unmapped future, might wither away? How important would curatorship, scheduling and the brand identity of individual channels continue to be? Would younger audiences in fact migrate back to more traditional modes of consumption as they got older, or was the game up for all that? Should the BBC follow its audiences out into the big wide world of the web, or try to usher them back into what Cooper called 'the walled garden' of the BBC?

Cooper, when we met in the summer of 2014 in his station's loft-like offices on the top floor of Broadcasting House, told me he believed Radio 1 should scatter its offerings in the places where people will find them. And so Radio 1 had established its own YouTube channel with 1.3 million subscribers, a third of them between thirteen and seventeen. On the channel you could find videos of performances and interviews: a paradoxical idea, perhaps, for a radio station, but a recognition of the visual, video-rich world that teenagers were inhabiting. (All the studios in Radio 1 had been fitted with cameras.) He had hired YouTube stars Dan and Phil as DJs – each had built up vast followings on their own YouTube channels – to tempt younger people to the BBC network. The strategy at Radio 1, Cooper said, in conscious echo of the tricolon 'inform, educate and entertain', was 'listen, watch, share'. It was, perhaps, a small way of acknowledging that the BBC, once the great distributor of material (you pressed the first button on the television and out poured BBC1, as if through a well-plumbed pipe), was now part of a world in which material circulates in much more unpredictable and uncontrollable ways, dragged hither and thither by the riptides, eddies and flows of the Internet. Cooper said he would like to add the word 'create' to that trio – and develop more ways of acting as a platform for his audi-ence's talent and ingeniousness.

Once the BBC was a giant. In 2014 it still was, if you looked at it in terms of its institutional size and its reach among British audiences in all its forms. But, seen from another angle, it was shrinking, fast. The online world is boundary-less and global, one in which the BBC was beginning to look rather small by comparison with the titans that were increasingly dominating it. According to James Purnell, the BBC's director of strategy and digital, 'At the time of the last charter review we were the same size as Apple. Apple's now twenty times bigger than the BBC. We were roughly the same size as Sky, they're now twice the size of us. BT wasn't in this market, but it is now, and BT is five times the size of BBC. We were 40 per cent of the broadcasting market in the UK. We're now down to 25 per cent.' 'The monoliths will shake,' Birt had warned in his outgoing speech as director general in 1999.

What does Reith's thinking look like in this context? Online, our lives, and our routes to BBC material, increasingly pass through the great ecosystems built by American conglomerates. Instead of pouring its programmes, as in the past, through pipes that it had either invented or whose development it had aided, it is obliged 'to play out its digital innovations in spaces that are essentially defined by Amazon, Google, Facebook and Apple', in the words of Matt Locke, a former head of innovation at BBC new media. For some, this is an inevitability, and the BBC has inherent qualities that will protect it and its audience. According to Rivera, 'Fragmentation is our friend, because we are the signal in the noise. The more that's out there, the more there is a need to go to places you trust that have high quality. And I believe when you have more choice there'll be more flight to quality because you don't have to accept mediocre or poor things.'

But maybe it does matter. If my life with the BBC has hitherto been about privacy – no one able to track my habits and predilections, no one able to sell me anything based on my desires – then perhaps it does make a difference if my path to BBC material online is both forged and tracked by these US corporate giants, and increasingly the BBC has to operate in ecosystems designed by those with profit-making motives far removed from their own founding civic principles. And if the BBC was not set up to be, precisely, radio or television or online, but, rather, at a more essential level, a great public space through whose generous and lofty halls we could all walk together as equals, outside the world of commerce, then maybe the BBC does have some kind of responsibility – 'big, even colossal', in the words of Reith. Some within the BBC believe that the future has already slipped out of the corporation's grasp: that it should have been at the forefront of guaranteeing access to public-service material online; it should have been inventing ways to protect security and privacy of personal data; it should have made its own browser, and its own Cloud-style storage. That there were more abstract, more searching questions to be asked – both by the corporation and the government – about how the BBC could fulfil a public-service destiny in the digital age. Hall's slant on such questions was to stress the importance of something that is 'owned here; is for Britain, and respects and reflects British values and the excitement of being British'.

The history of the BBC is, of course, not just the history of the institution and its output; it is the history of how its audience has received it. Matt Locke spoke to me of what he called 'patterns of attention'. Talking to him made me think about how our attentiveness – our ways of paying attention – to the BBC has changed over the past 92 years. In the 1930 BBC Handbook, advice was given on how best to appreciate the wireless: 'Listen as carefully at home as you do in a theatre or concert hall. You can't get the best out of a programme if your mind is wandering, or if you are playing bridge or reading. Give it your full attention. Try turning out the lights so that your eye is not caught by familiar objects in the room. Your imagination will be twice as vivid.' Sir David Attenborough told me of his early years in television in the 1950s, when the evening 'programme' (then meaning not an individual show, but, as it were, the whole evening's playbill) was organised in the expectation that you would sit down and watch 'the lot. And so consequently the schedule was like making a meal, starting with something little, a little frippery, an hors d'oeuvre and maybe an indication of what might be coming in the evening; and then you had the main course, which was a play or something serious, and then, to end it all, you had a religious blessing – certainly on a Sunday.' In the very early days viewers were perfectly prepared to telephone the programme-makers while a show was still going out to demand, if they thought it was dragging, that they 'get on with it'.

All of this has changed, of course: radio has become something we might listen to while driving or cooking or working. We do not automatically gather before the television from 7.30 to 10.30 p.m., fearful that if we don't watch the whole lot we aren't getting our money's worth. If we do sit down in front of it at an appointed moment, and most of us still do, we might be tweeting about it at the same time, or following a liveblog, involved in a discussion about it that goes far beyond our own living room. Television now seems at its most powerful, in fact, when we sit down to watch live events whose outcome we will observe in real time, such as a football match – looping back, in a sense, to the qualities early identified as the form's most exciting characteristics. As early as 1923, in the *Radio Times* of 19 October, an article talked about the coming technology of television. 'The transmission of sound by wireless, only a few years ago a scientist's dream, is now an everyday fact,' proclaimed the article. 'An even more marvellous thing will soon by possible . . . Mr Jones will be able to sit comfortably in his own parlour on Derby Day and watch his favourite romping home – last! . . . No more special trains for the Cup Tie need be run! The match will be watched by the various supporters in the television apparatus.'

How will we pay attention in the future? What part will the BBC play in our lives? Will the tread of the new giants – BT and Netflix and Amazon – crush the BBC underfoot? Will the government support or punish the BBC, simultaneously over-mighty and shrinking as it is? Will the BBC itself successfully remake its public-service mission for an Internet age? Like the early pioneers of the BBC we stand at a great junction in the ages of communication. Hilda

Matheson talked about the generation beneath her much as those of us above a certain age describe, with a certain wonderment, 'digital natives'. 'The child born at the same time as broadcasting takes it so much for granted that he can scarcely think of a pre-broadcasting age,' she wrote. 'He is apt to think of it as having always existed, as much "always" in his world as motor cars, gramophones and aeroplanes.'

Matheson and the other early pioneers saw no end to the possibilities of broadcasting. They were utopian in their fantasies. It is their optimism and fearlessness that our BBC needs now. It is clear-sighted and subtle political wisdom that is needed now, too, not grandstanding and playing to the gallery. Ninety years ago, Arthur Burrows asked, 'What surprises may be in store on the other side of silence? How far will our present knowledge of music prepare us for an appreciation of nature's eternal harmonies – the seasonal cadences of the rising and falling sap, the music of the growing grass and the love songs of butterflies?' Lambert summed up the hopes of that eager post-war generation: 'All kinds of petty discomforts – overcrowded rooms, long hours, arbitrary or tactless treatment – were overlooked in the general sense of adventure, progress, and public service. You felt it a privilege to be "in" at the birth of such a mighty experiment – an experiment not merely in the use of a new invention, broadcasting, but in its use for communal ends, rather than for private profit. Who could tell how far the new service would go?'

11

Conclusion: Welcome to the BBC

It was a hot London day, and the U-shaped courtyard of the BBC in Portland Place was airless and sun-strafed. Light glared off pale stone. Employees crowded into a sliver of shade to eat their lunchtime sandwiches. The doors of the older, 1930s wing stood open, so that the wonky, stained little notice that sometimes hangs there bidding visitors 'Welcome to the BBC', was invisible. On my many visits, I had enjoyed this intimate, ad-hoc sign. It was so different from the portentous portals of its neighbour, New Broadcasting House, opened in 2013, where there was nothing so improvised and human as this. Nor yet was there any poetic challenge to the soul, no Latin inscription proclaiming this as a temple of the arts, as there was in the foyer of the older building. Instead, images of BBC personalities – a procession of men – hung above the reception desk: actors Benedict Cumberbatch and Martin Freeman in *Sherlock* guise; Idris Elba as Luther; and physicist Brian Cox staring soulfully into the horizon.

I sat in the foyer of New Broadcasting House, watching the ebb and flow of staff as they made their exits and entrances, among the other visitors waiting to be ushered beyond a set of revolving doors into the inner chambers. Once there, suddenly illuminated by an uncanny reddish glow, you could look down into the newsroom thrumming

Broadcasting House reborn. Much enlarged, it reopened in 2013.

away below you in the basement, or cast your eye upwards to the glass walls that rise above. The newsroom should have had columns like great trees supporting it, according to the original vision of the architect, Sir Richard MacCormac, but along the way – and amid acrimony – the corporation dropped this flourish on budgetary grounds. The BBC's principal building seemed to me to resemble the institution itself – the new and the old tangled together in uncertain harmony; high artistic ambitions sometimes compromised; a certain corporate pomposity undercut by small, humane gestures.

How healthy is the BBC of today? Will it flourish for another hundred years, and another? As I sat in the foyer, staff passes cheeping their way through the security barriers, I considered what I had learned about this corporation over the past nine months. It was, in fact, ungraspable in its entirety: it was like a city whose streets I had only partially explored, a place whose streetscape was so circuitous and complex that a lifetime would be too short to map it. I had met many people within these labyrinthine alleys who were admirable and clever and kind. I had also found something less attractive: a subtle atmosphere that seemed to emanate from the BBC that was difficult to describe and surely unconscious. A collective sense of superiority, perhaps? The *Guardian*, my employer, had never felt small to me before I started writing about the BBC.

What had surprised me was the BBC's vulnerability. It may be great in size, but is blasted and buffeted on every side by powerful and ruthless enemies. Every move of the BBC is monitored, analysed, discussed. A cadre of Fleet Street journalists exists solely to examine it. And yet the passions roused by the BBC are so intense precisely because all of us have a relationship with it: 96 per cent of us use it, including, of course, its most vituperative detractors. It is with us in our homes, our cars, our phones, our computer screens; it is our omnipresent, intimate companion. It speaks to us benignly, amiably. Reith wrote in 1924 that the voices on the BBC were 'the friends of the people of these islands, and have come to be so accepted . . .'

Our relationship with the BBC has changed in recent years. It is not, as it once was, a cathedral in which we all gather together, but, rather, a many-roomed palace in which we are free to roam, where we will encounter others with whom to marvel at its riches, but through which we will none the less choose our own route, pace and narrative. Despite this increasingly fragmented experience, for most of us the BBC is the national institution that most powerfully touches our inner lives – working its way into our sense of ourselves as individuals and as part of a community, our convictions, our imaginations. And if the screen is a kind of mirror into which the nation gazes, we are often in sharp disagreement about the accuracy of the reflection it throws back. The BBC is a space in which the most fundamental anxieties about cultural identity and political purpose can be fought out – often bitterly.

Arguably, the old *Mail* taunt that the BBC was a nest of liberals, with an institutionalised left-wing bias, looked more and more difficult to sustain during the time that I was researching the institution. Indeed there were fears on the centre left that the BBC had consciously or unconsciously drifted to the right, exhausted by the daily clamouring of its noisiest critics, and no longer quite held the impartial centre. There were fears too that, still bruised a decade on after its wrestling match with the last government over its coverage of the run-up to the Iraq war – a bout that ended with the resignation of both its director general, Greg Dyke, and its chairman, Gavyn Davies – the BBC could be pusillanimous in some of its reporting. It has feared to challenge – and when its journalists did so, as with Meirion Jones's and Liz MacKean's investigation into Jimmy Savile, it was capable of self-sabotage. The BBC that withstood a 36-hour raid of its Glasgow headquarters by Special Branch in the 1980s over the Zircon affair (an investigation into a £500 million spy satellite whose existence was unknown to the Public Accounts Committee) felt like a distant memory to these critics, who would adumbrate the corporation's reaction to the revelations in 2013–14 by former NSA employee Edward Snowden.

In the US; in Australia; in mainland Europe, especially Germany; in Asia, especially Indonesia; and in Latin America, especially Brazil and Mexico, the information leaked concerning Prism and Tempora – the secret programmes used for mass surveillance of email communication in the US and UK respectively – was treated with real seriousness and provoked urgent public debate. The *New York Times* and the *Washington Post* regarded the story as of global significance; so did *Channel 4 News*. But *Channel 4 News* is, in the words of its editor, 'an ant versus Goliath when it comes to the BBC', with an audience of around 650,000. The BBC – which by virtue of its sheer scale holds the ring of national debate – remained almost mute. And so it was that, of all the nations in the world, it was on its home turf that the *Guardian*, which had broken the Snowden story, remained virtually a lone voice. Meanwhile, its editor Alan Rusbridger was asked to prove his patriotism before a committee of MPs, and GCHQ operatives arrived at the organisation's offices to supervise the destruction of computer hard drives.

The charge of pusillanimity was denied by Tony Hall. 'I don't recognise that picture at all,' he said. 'The fact is – and this is one of the things I know about impartiality – when people know a lot about a story, they kick up a big fuss because we're not reporting it as they want us to report it. But then part of our job is to stand back from the furore and say actually let's put this in context, let's do this properly. In that instance I don't see any pulling back at all.' Hall added, 'One of the things that has always amazed me about the BBC is that it is the most self-questioning organisation I've ever worked in. It asks itself questions all the time about whether it's doing the right thing, could we have done that better.' In other words, his conscience was clear.

When I asked James Harding some weeks earlier whether he would have run with the Snowden story had it come directly to him, he argued that the issue was not that it touched on such delicate matters of state – but rather that it was, he claimed, a piece of campaigning journalism that was invested in a particular outcome:

I don't think the issue would have been whether the BBC could have gone after a story about the behaviour of a different part of the state – of a part of the state, sorry . . . That's what you do if you cover the NHS, if you cover the police, if you cover the armed forces, if you cover the intelligence services . . . I don't think that's an issue at all. I think the thing that is really tricky on Snowden is where you get yourself straddling a line between reporting a story and campaigning a story.

Now we obviously cannot campaign. We cannot use the public's money to make an argument. And the nature of that kind of leak and that kind of story was that the person who held the information wanted a certain story and to roll it out in a certain way. That deal, the deal between, if you like, the media organisation and the source – I'm not sure we could have done that deal . . . So in my last job [as editor of *The Times*] I ran a campaign on something as, you may think as innocuous as cycling safety. You couldn't campaign on cycling safety at the BBC. And that's where things are different.

However, there was no deal between the *Guardian* and Snowden to give the story a particular angle or to campaign for a particular set of outcomes. Nor indeed did Snowden himself bring a particular agenda to his whistleblowing beyond wishing to allow the public to enter a debate – as he put it, to 'give society the chance to determine if it wanted to change itself'. The analogy drawn between the Snowden whistleblowing and the *Times*'s (entirely laudable) cycling campaign seemed to me to be infelicitous. The more I thought about BBC news, the more I wondered whether it really was the corporation's impartiality or drift to the political right or left that was the central problem. Rather, in the end I began to feel that it was, in its very bones, an organisation that found it difficult to challenge the most sensitive parts of the British establishment (often despite the most vigorous attempts of its own journalists) – precisely because it was a part of the establishment.

If journalism is at the heart of the BBC, the thing above all by which it stands or falls, its television drama is what most of us think of when we think of our own enjoyment of the BBC. When we spoke in 2014, Hall talked proudly of the commissioning of a second tranche of Shakespeare history plays, a follow-up to the highly acclaimed *Hollow*

Crown season of 2012, for which Sam Mendes executive-produced films of *Richard II*, *Henry IV Parts I* and *II*, and *Henry V*. Sir Richard Eyre directed the two *Henry IV* plays. In fact, he regarded the whole episode with a certain scepticism, he told me. The commission was generated not by an enthusiastic drama department, he said, but 'by fiat' from the then director general Mark Thompson, who decided that a strong cultural statement ought to be made by the BBC in the year of the London Olympics. 'It was not a popular idea [within the BBC]. I had absolutely nothing to do with the BBC at all until it was made,' he said. 'When I had a fine cut of my two films, I said I was going to show them on successive days at a preview theatre. And I couldn't get anybody from the BBC to come. They asked me to send tapes over to them. I said, "No. I've worked for a year on these, come to a preview theatre, watch it on the screen and then we'll discuss it afterwards." Then much to their surprise it was very well received and people were saying, "Now we understand what the BBC does; this is the jewel in the crown of the BBC." He laughed. 'Suddenly they were running after us.'

Michael Grade, once a controller of BBC1, later BBC chairman, told me he believed that 'process' had muffled the commissioning power of the old BBC impresarios, the television 'barons' of yesteryear who had enormous power but who stood or fell by the quality of their shows. 'Today you don't know who's responsible for anything. It's so convoluted, the system . . . Committees, eight signatures, e-submission, I mean what's going on? It should be all about editorship, about somebody owning the product in each area, and having the vision, and if they're no good, if their batting average is not up to snuff, sorry chum, we'll get the next one in.' I spoke to James Graham, who writes for theatre (his play *This House* was a major success for the National Theatre) as well as for BBC radio and television. Things were changing vastly for the better, he told me, but 'I remember when I began a feeling of impossibility of ever getting anything on. And I knew people who'd made a living out of just developing TV that would never see the light of day and never get beyond a certain stage.'

For example, several years previously he had spent a year developing a script for the BBC about young Western travellers in Thailand, including spending time in the country. The script went back and forth endlessly, working its way through many drafts. Finally, 'staff were rotating, executives were moving to different places, and it lost momentum. And I don't even know if anyone has ever turned it down' – but it quietly died. The process was enervating: 'I'd rather have been working in bars and writing plays that were definitely going to be made than spending all my time and energy on something that just never felt like it was going to happen.' The development process used 'to feel a bit like a computer game. It was as if you had to pass all these different levels and these different baddies before you get to the big baddy at the end.'

Andrew O'Hagan, the novelist, essayist and playwright told me he felt a quiet despair at the commissioning process even for BBC radio – which operates as a structured, staged, submission process taking several months from idea to green light. 'The relationship between the "talent" and the broadcaster has become deranged. The pitching process has the effect of killing the thing you love; and because of that the BBC is falling out of touch with a whole generation of writers,' he said. He compared the process with that on magazines such as the *New Yorker*, where editors are strongly empowered curators, forging relationships with writers, constantly questing outwards for new ideas; or indeed the commissioning process in British theatre. 'A clever commissioner should be trusted to make the programmes they want to make,' he said.

Bound up with the complaint of byzantine process and bureaucracy was a continued sense of disenfranchisement between the BBC's worker class – including many of its news reporters – and its executives. 'I think the over-remuneration of people [under former director general Mark Thompson] was a huge mistake,' foreign correspondent Jeremy Bowen told me when we met between his trips to Syria in the spring of 2014. 'It's caused massive damage to the BBC. It's caused it internally, because the vast majority of people who work at the BBC do not get brilliantly paid. But the massive salaries given to top management angered people on the shop floor, exaggerated the "them and us" feeling that there was a chauffeur-driven top of the corporation with enormous salaries and massive bonuses. And that caused a lot of resentment and still does. I resented it personally.'

Such problems were hampering the articulation of the case to be made about the particular and precious qualities of the BBC, and indeed the whole of the public-service broadcasting system in the UK – a protective and protected arena in the public realm, a space where the intangible collective experience was prized for its own sake and in which there was a different value system in play than that of the vast, and growing, American conglomerates. Dennis Potter, in his 1993 MacTaggart lecture, said, remembering his childhood relationship with the BBC:

> More than the coming of the bus and the train or even the daily newspaper, it was the voices out of the air which, as though by magic, pushed out [the] constricting boundaries [of my childhood]. You could hear a play that made the back of your neck tingle as well as a dance band that made your foot tap, a brow-furrowing talk about something I'd never heard of as well as an I-say I-say I-say music-hall routine, or even (and how bizarre) a ventriloquist's dummy as well as a not wholly dissimilar newsreader. And none of it was trying to sell you anything.

I began to think of the BBC as if it were a church: supported by high ideals, feeding our inner lives, sustained by the goodwill of the faithful, and, sometimes – like all large institutions – infuriating in its internal workings. 'Sustained by the goodwill of the faithful' is the most important part of that: the licence fee is remarkably well tolerated because the British public still recognises the BBC as one of the greatest institutions of Britain, something that almost defines Britishness both at home and abroad, a national broadcaster that is still the envy of the world, an institution that, for all its problems and peccadilloes, is part of us, the shining, hypnotic screen into which we look and see ourselves, the collector of our memories and the gleaner of our experience. It is a survivor from another age – it is hard for me not to betray myself and write a better age – when the notion of a technological advancement being harnessed for the democratic benefit of the commonweal was not a fanciful one, when calling the BBC *templum artium*, a temple of the arts, was not faintly embarrassing. As Michael Grade put it: 'You wouldn't invent a hereditary monarchy today; you wouldn't invent the House of Lords; you wouldn't invent the BBC in a dynamic market. You either believe in it or you don't. You can't intellectually – in a modern sense with a modern mindset – justify it. But it is part of what makes this country different from anywhere else in the world. And you either believe in the BBC or you don't: the BBC is essentially an idea.'

Without the BBC we would be poorer in spirit. We would know less about the world: our cultural, musical, political lives would be diminished, our curiosity neither so piqued nor so sated. It threads itself through all our lives. The BBC, in my view, was unquestionably worth fighting for, worth preserving and worth championing. It was worth defending despite all its myriad flaws, flaws that the BBC ought to be better at acknowledging and solving, flaws that its audience and critics ought to be able to discuss subtly, without bullying and hysteria. The BBC needs constantly to reinvent itself; like a church, it must earn, and cannot wholly take for granted, the patience of the faithful. Those who love it expect much from it: we expect more from it. We cheer it on, but we urge it to do better. We still believe. We do not wish to see it stumble. We do not wish to hear its melancholy, long, withdrawing roar.

A Note on Sources

Much of the research for this book was gleaned through interviews with BBC employees past and present and those who know the organisation well. When directly quoted, subjects are named except in the rare cases when individuals chose to speak off the record.

As I was finishing the project, too late to be of use to me, an important resource was made available by the BBC: a searchable archive of *Radio Times* listings at http://genome.ch.bbc.co.uk.

1 Reith of the BBC

The key reading matter here is *The Birth of Broadcasting* (1961) the first volume of Asa Briggs's *The History of Broadcasting in the United Kingdom*. Reith's autobiography *Into the Wind* (1949) sketches out his early life, and his *Broadcast Over Britain* (1924) is a key statement of early BBC ideology. Ian McIntyre's *The Expense of Glory: A Life of John Reith* (1993) reveals much of the darker side of the first director general. *The Reith Diaries* (1979), edited by Charles Stuart, are a heavily compressed volume of the man's vast daily output. The Crawford Parliamentary

Report of 1925 gives a crucial account of political thinking on the BBC.

Malcolm Muggeridge's interviews with Reith, filmed for BBC2 in 1967, are held in the BBC archive. They give a vivid sense of the former DG's looming presence and unquiet mind.

2 'People, telephones, alarms, excursions': Hilda Matheson

Eric Maschwitz's often hilarious account of the BBC's Savoy Hill years is in his memoir *No Chip on My Shoulder* (1957). The recollections of Matheson by Lionel Fielden come from his rather whimsical memoir *The Natural Bent* (1960). He also wrote an account of her for her obituary volume *Hilda Matheson* (no editor credited) – a slim book with a small print run published by the Hogarth Press, fairly hard to track down but readable in the London School of Economics library. From this volume come the memories of her mother, her Oxford tutor Lettice Fisher and Nancy Astor as well as those of H. G. Wells and Ethyl Smyth. Richard Lambert's book A*riel and All His Quality* (1940) contains a sympathetic sketch of Matheson.

Her own words come from three main sources. First, her delightful, earnest and wise 1933 book *Broadcasting*, which she wrote after leaving the BBC. Second, the many bureaucratic traces (memos and letters) that she left, now held by the Corporation's Written Archives Centre. Third and most vivid is her copious correspondence with Vita Sackville-West. Her letters are now held by the Beinecke

Rare Book and Manuscript Library at the University of Yale. Extracts are reproduced by kind permission of the Vita Sackville-West estate.

The most important secondary sources on Matheson are *Stoker* (1999), a biography by Michael Carney; and Kate Murphy's PhD thesis, "'On an Equal Footing with Men?': Women and Work at the BBC, 1923–1939' (2011). The last is available online.

3 Inform, educate, entertain

Eric Maschwitz's *No Chip on My Shoulder* (1957) is again useful for its lively evocation of the Savoy Hill years. Arthur Burrows's *The Story of Broadcasting* and Cecil Lewis's *Broadcasting From Within* (both 1924) were written more or less on the spot. The Grierson film is available via the British Film Institute DVD box set *Addressing the Nation: The GPO Film Unit Collection, Volume 1* or else in libraries through screenonline.org.

The main sources on Edward Clark are his voluminous and often startling personal file in the BBC Written Archives Centre, and Jenny Doctor's scholarly work *The BBC and Ultra-modern Music, 1922–1936* (1999). Elisabeth Lutyens's autobiography *A Goldfish Bowl* (1972) includes a sketch of her husband (though she fails to mention his son or first marriage) and the biography of Lutyens by M. and S. Harries, *A Pilgrim Soul* (1989), has further details. I am grateful to Dr Doctor for giving me a long and generous interview about Clark in particular and musical conditions in the early BBC in general.

It was my brother Rupert Higgins who first mentioned Ludwig Koch's autobiography *Memoirs of a Birdman* (1955) to me. From his description it was a short leap to realising that Penelope Fitzgerald had based her character Dr Vogel ('Dr Bird') on him in her elegant BBC novel *Human Voices* (1980). Koch left a fascinating trail in the BBC Written Archives Centre (mostly vigorously conducted disputes about fees and time expended on projects), and a number of his programmes, as well as interviews with him, can be heard in the National Sound Archives at the British Library. There is a 2009 Radio 4 documentary about his work, *Ludwig Koch and the Music of Nature*, available on the BBC website.

Lew Grade's autobiography *Still Dancing* (1988) conveys how the Winogradsky brothers rose from being impoverished East Enders to giants of show business. His nephew Michael Grade's autobiography *It Seemed Like a Good Idea at the Time* (1989) is also useful.

The point about the alternative comedians of the early 1980s being sought out by the BBC's head of light entertainment for BBC2 is made in Louis Barfe's *Turned Out Nice Again* (2009).

For the paragraphs on *The Great War*, I drew on an interview with and a paper by Taylor Wilding. The paper was given at the Science Museum in April 2014 as part of 'BBC2: Origin, Influence, Audiences – a 50th Anniversary Conference'. There is a selection of interviews extracted from the programmes ('The Great War Interviews') available on BBC iPlayer and episodes can be seen on YouTube.

Work by Adam Curtis can be seen at bbc.co.uk/
blogs/adamcurtis.

Texts for all the previous MacTaggart lectures, including
Dennis Potter's, are available at the Guardian Edinburgh
Television Festival website: http://www.geitf.co.uk/GEITF/
mactaggart-hall-of-fame.

Matheson's recollection at the end of the chapter is
found in *Broadcasting* (1933).

4 'Television is a bomb about to burst': Grace Wyndham Goldie

The first port of call on Grace Wyndham Goldie is her
own book on politics and broadcasting, *Facing the Nation*
(1977), which also includes memories of working at
Alexandra Palace. Her key early writings on the power of
television are 'Viewing Television' in the *Listener* of 16
June 1937 and a chapter entitled 'Television', in *Made for
Millions* (1947). Her criticism can be read ad libitum in
1930s editions of the *Listener* – assuming you aren't
sidetracked by fiction reviews by E. M. Forster, stories by
Elizabeth Bowen and other myriad delights.

For her detailed memories and well-articulated views
on broadcasting there are also three long interviews conducted with her as part of the BBC's oral-history holdings,
covering her entire life and career as a critic, a civil servant,
in BBC radio and finally in television. They were conducted by Tony Trebble, Huw Wheldon and Frank Gillard
in 1977. My thanks to Robert Seatter and his colleagues
in the BBC history department for making transcripts

available. Material is reproduced by kind permission of the Grace Wyndham Goldie Trust. Unless otherwise stated, quotations from Wyndham Goldie in this chapter derive from these interviews.

The BBC Written Archives hold plentiful material on Wyndham Goldie, including a well-stocked file on the televising of the 1950 general election that encompasses memos, scripts and set layouts. Material was also gleaned from the WAC file on *Tonight*. Dr David Butler's aptitude for television is described in *Facing the Nation*; the man himself very kindly shared his memories of the night of the 1950 election with me in person. John Grist is the author of a biography, *Grace Wyndham Goldie* (2006), which draws on his own memories of working for her as well as archive material and her correspondence with her husband Frank (the last not consulted directly by me).

Goldie crops up in the autobiographies of those who worked for her, including Alasdair Milne's *DG* (1988), David Attenborough's *Life on Air* (2003) and Woodrow Wyatt's *Confessions of an Optimist* (1985). Antony Jay's memories of *Tonight* come from an episode of the BBC Radio 4 programme *The Reunion* first broadcast on 2 May 2010, and available on the BBC website.

5 The great, the good and the damned

Former directors general like to write their memoirs. Of most use in this chapter were Reith's *Into the Wind* (1949), Birt's *The Harder Path* (2002), and Hugh Carleton Greene's *The Third Floor Front* (1969). The last is not so much a memoir as a collection of speeches and writings. Birt's outgoing lecture as DG, 'The Prize and the Price', given under the auspices of the *New Statesman* at Banqueting House in Whitehall on 6 July 1999, is a fascinating and revealing document. Hugh Carleton Greene's *Desert Island Discs* can be heard on the BBC website. Balancing Birt's account of his own tenure is a fascinating anthropological study of the BBC conducted over the period when his reforms were being enacted: Georgina Born's *Uncertain Vision* (2004). A highly entertaining view, clearly sourced from journalists working under the new regime, is Chris Horrie's and Steve Clarke's *Fuzzy Monsters* (1994).

6 'A spot of bother'

Alasdair Milne's own account of his director-generalship, *DG* (1988), gives his version of the *Real Lives* scandal. My colleague Lisa O'Carroll is the author of a fascinating article, 'The Truth Behind *Real Lives*', published on the *Guardian* website on 12 December 2005. The piece contains links to relevant documents including the minutes of governors' meetings and the home secretary's and chairman's correspondence. A clear narrative of the events at *Newsnight* in 2012 is given by Vin Ray in *Is the BBC in Crisis?* (2013), edited by John Mair et al.

7 Independent and Impartial?

Anne Perkins's book *A Very British Strike* (2006) gives a vivid day-by-day account of the General Strike. Reith's own part in it is told in his diaries – though they were not written by the day, but after the strike had ended. The third volume of Virginia Woolf's diaries, edited by A. O. Bell (1982), gives the view from Bloomsbury. Hilda Matheson's *Broadcasting* (1933) and Richard Lambert's *Ariel and All His Quality* (1940) contain assessments of the BBC's role. Marcia Williams's assessment of Harold Wilson's views on the BBC is in her *Inside Number 10* (1972).

8 Enemies at the Gate

Paul Dacre's 2007 Cudlipp lecture, which makes for striking reading, can be found in full on the *Guardian* website. Peter Eckersley's *The Power Behind the Microphone* (1941) is by turns revealing, angry and fascinating. The biography *Prospero's Wireless* (1998), by his son Myles Eckersley, is also intriguing. The BBC Written Archives Centre is also a source of much material on this extraordinary man. Martin Le Jeune's *To Inform, Educate and Entertain?* (2009) gives a useful account of objections to the BBC from a free-market perspective. *Beyond the Charter* (2004) by David Elstein et al. is also a useful critical document.

9 'The great globe itself'

Jon Day's essay 'Time and the City' inspired some of the ideas of the opening paragraphs of the chapter. The letter from the listener in Malaysia is quoted by Dr Emma Robertson in her essay "'I Get a Real Kick out of Big Ben": BBC Versions of Britishness on the Empire and General

Overseas Service, 1932–1948' (2008). Hilda Matheson's thoughts on 'standard English' are in *Broadcasting* (1933). Linda Colley's *Acts of Union and Disunion* (2014), based on a series of essays for BBC radio, is a useful and highly readable primer on the historical forces at work on ideas of Britishness. The second volume of Asa Briggs's *The History of Broadcasting in the United Kingdom*, *The Golden Age of Wireless* (1965), explains the beginnings of overseas broadcasting and the pressures on regional broadcasting. Alban Webb's book *London Calling* (2014) has much of interest to say about the purpose and significance of overseas broadcasting after the war. Excerpts from Olive Shapley's remarkable memoir, including an account of her back-street abortion, are published in Caroline Mitchell's *Women and Radio* (2000). Eckersley's trenchant views on regional broadcasting are found in *The Power Behind the Microphone* (1941). No archive recording of Auden's *On Hadrian's Wall* exists but the playscript can be found in the first volume of his collected works, edited by Edward Mendelson (1988). Details about the birth of Radio Stoke were gleaned from an article on the BBC website, 'History of Radio Stoke'.

10 'The monoliths will shake'

The sense of the unknown, the sense of adventure in the early days of the BBC is conveyed in many accounts – Reith's *Into The Wind* (1949) and *Broadcast Over Britain* (1924), Eric Maschwitz's *No Chip on My Shoulder* (1957), Arthur Burrows's *The Story of Broadcasting* (1924), Hilda

Matheson's *Broadcasting* (1933), Cecil Lewis's *Broadcasting From Within* (1924) and Richard Lambert's *Ariel and All His Quality* (1940). Peter Eckersley's vision of a multi-channel future is in *The Power Behind the Microphone* (1941).

Select Bibliography

Anon (ed.), *Hilda Matheson: Born June 7, died October 20, 1940*, Letchworth, 1940

Attenborough, D., *Life on Air: Memoirs of a Broadcaster*, London, 2003

Avery, T., *Radio Modernism: Literature, Ethics, and the BBC, 1922–1938*, Aldershot, 2006

Bakewell, J., *The Centre of the Bed*, London, 2004

Bakewell, J., and N. Garnham, *The New Priesthood: British Television Today*, London, 1970

Banks-Smith, N., 'Cause and Bloody Effect', *Guardian*, 17 October 1985

Barfe, L., *Turned Out Nice Again: The Story of British Light Entertainment*, 2nd edn, London, 2009

Barnett, S., and A. Curry, *The Battle for the BBC: A British Broadcasting Conspiracy*, London, 1994

Barwise, P., and R. G. Picard, 'What If There Were No BBC Television: The Net Impact on UK Viewers', from the project Public Service Broadcasting in a Digital World, Oxford, 2014

Bell, A. O. (ed.), *The Diary of Virginia Woolf, Volume III: 1925–30*, Harmondsworth, 1982

Birt, J., 'The Prize and the Price: The Social, Political and Cultural Consequences of the Digital Age', The New Statesman Media Lecture, 6 July 1999

— *The Harder Path: The Autobiography*, London, 2002

— 'Scottish Independence Would Have a Devastating Effect on the BBC', theguardian.com, 19 August 2014

Born, G., *Uncertain Vision: Birt, Dyke and the Reinvention of the BBC*, London, 2004

Briggs, A., *The History of Broadcasting in the United Kingdom*, vols 1–5, Oxford, 1961–95

— *The BBC: The First 50 Years*, Oxford, 1985

Burnett, G., *Scotland on the Air: Descriptions of the Working of Various BBC Departments in Scotland by the Officials in Charge of Them*, Moray, 1938

Burns, T., *The BBC: Public Institution and Private World*, London, 1977

Burrows, A. R., *The Story of Broadcasting*, London, 1924

Buscombe, E. (ed.), *A British Television Reader*, Oxford, 2000

Carney, M., *Stoker: The Life of Hilda Matheson OBE*, Pencaedu, 1999

Carpenter, H., with J. Doctor, *The Envy of the World: 50 Years of the Third Programme and Radio 3, 1946–1996*, London, 1996

Colley, L., *Acts of Union and Disunion: What Has Held the UK Together, and What is Dividing It?*, London, 2014

Cotton, B., *Double Bill*, London, 2000

Crisell, A., *An Introductory History of British Broadcasting*, 2nd edn, London, 2002

Curran, J., and J. Seaton, *Power Without Responsibility: The Press, Broadcasting and New Media in Britain*, 6th edn, London, 2003

Day, J., 'Time and the City', thejunket.org, 25 April 2014

Day, R., *Day by Day: A Dose of My Own Hemlock*, London, 1975

— *Grand Inquisitor*, London, 1989

Dimbleby, J., *Richard Dimbleby*, Sevenoaks, 1977

Doctor, J., *The BBC and Ultra-modern Music, 1922–1936*, Cambridge, 1999

Downing, T., *The World at War* (BFI TV Classics), London, 2012

Drummond, J., *Tainted by Experience: A Life in the Arts*, London, 2000

Eckersley, M., *Prospero's Wireless: P. P. Eckersley*, Romsey, rev. edn, 1998

Eckersley, P. P., *The Power Behind the Microphone*, London, 1941

Edgar, D., 'What Are We Telling the Nation?', *London Review of Books*, 7 July 2005

Elstein, D., D. Cox, B. Donoghue, D. Graham and D. Metzger, *Beyond the Charter: The BBC after 2006*, London, 2004

Fielden, L., *The Natural Bent*, London, 1960

Fitzgerald, P., *Human Voices*, London, 1980

Frith, S., 'The Pleasures of the Hearth: The Making of BBC Light Entertainment', in S. Watney (ed.), *Formations of Pleasure*, London, 1983

Gillespie, M., and A. Webb (eds.), *Disapora and Diplomacy: Cosmopolitan Contact Zones at the BBC World Service (1932–2012)*, London, 2013

Glock, W., 'The BBC's Music Policy', BBC Lunchtime Lecture, London, 1963

—*Notes in Advance*, Oxford, 1991

Grade, L., *Still Dancing: My Story*, London, 1988

Grade, M., *It Seemed Like a Good Idea at the Time*, London, 1989

Greene, H., *The Third Floor Front, A View of Broadcasting in the Sixties*, London, 1969

Grist, J., *Grace Wyndham Goldie: First Lady of Television*, Sandy, 2006

Harries, M., and S. Harries, *A Pilgrim Soul: The Life and Work of Elisabeth Lutyens*, London, 1989

Hendy, D., *Life on Air: A History of Radio Four*, Oxford, 2007

Hines, M., *The Story of Broadcasting House, Home of the BBC*, London, 2008

Horrie, C., and S. Clarke, *Fuzzy Monsters: Fear and Loathing at the BBC*, London, 1994

Hunter, F., 'Hilda Matheson and the BBC, 1926–1940', in S. Oldfield (ed.), *This Working Day World: Women's Lives and Cultures in Britain*, London, 1994, pp. 169–74

Kenyon, N., *The BBC Symphony Orchestra: The First 50 Years, 1930–1980*, London, 1981

Koch, L., *Memoirs of a Birdman*, London, 1955

Lambert, R. S., *Ariel and All His Quality: An Impression of the BBC from Within*, London, 1940

Lean, T., *Voices in the Darkness*, London, 1943

Lee, H., *Penelope Fitzgerald: A Life*, London, 2013

Le Jeune, M., *To Inform, Educate and Entertain? British Broadcasting in the Twenty-first Century*, London, 2009

Lewis, C. A., *Broadcasting From Within*, London, 1924

Lutyens, E., *A Goldfish Bowl*, London, 1972

Nicolson, N., (ed.), *The Harold Nicolson Diaries, 1907–1963*, London, 2004

MacGregor, S., *Woman of Today*, London 2002

McIntyre, I., *The Expense of Glory: A Life of John Reith*, London, 1993

Mair, J., R. Tait and R. L. Keeble (eds.), *Is the BBC in Crisis?*, Bury St Edmunds, 2013

Mansell, G., *Let Truth Be Told: 50 Years of BBC External Broadcasting*, London, 1982

Maschwitz, E., *No Chip on My Shoulder*, London, 1957

Matheson, H., *Broadcasting*, London, 1933

Mayhew, C., *Time to Explain*, London, 1987

Milne, A., *DG: The Memoirs of a British Broadcaster*, London, 1988

Mitchell, C., *Women and Radio: Airing Differences*, London, 2000

Moran, J., *Armchair Nation: An Intimate History of Britain in Front of the TV*, London, 2013

Muggeridge, M., *The Thirties*, London, 1940 (paperback edn, 1989)

Murphy, C., '"On an Equal Footing with Men?" Women and Work at the BBC, 1923–1939', doctoral thesis, Goldsmiths, University of London, 2011

O'Carroll, L., 'The Truth Behind *Real Lives*', theguardian.com, 12 December 2005

O'Hagan, A., 'Light Entertainment', *London Review of Books*, 8 November 2012

Perkins, A., *A Very British Strike*, London, 2006

Purnell, J., 'The BBC Should Learn from the Birt Era', *Financial Times*, 13 November 2012

Reith, J., *Broadcast Over Britain*, London, 1924

— *Into the Wind*, London, 1949

Robertson, E., '"I Get a Real Kick out of Big Ben": BBC Versions of Britishness on the Empire and General Overseas Service, 1932–1948', *Historical Journal of Film, Radio and Television* 28 (4), 2008

Rolo, C. J., *Radio Goes to War*, London, 1943

Saltire Society, *Broadcasting: A Policy for Future Development*, Edinburgh, 1944

Scannell, P., and D. Cardiff, *A Social History of British Broadcasting, Volume 1: 1922–39*, Oxford, 1991

Schlesinger, P., D. Miller and W. Dinan, *Open Scotland? Journalists, Spin Doctors and Lobbyists*, Edinburgh, 2001

Stuart, C. (ed.), *The Reith Diaries*, London, 1979

Trethowan, I., *Split Screen*, London, 1984

Tusa, J., *A World in Your Ear*, London, 1992

Webb, A., *London Calling: Britain, the BBC World Service and the Cold War*, London, 2014

West, W. J., *Truth Betrayed*, London, 1987

Williams, M., *Inside Number 10*, London, 1972

Williams, R., *Television: Technology and Cultural Form*, London, 1990

Wyatt, Will, *The Fun Factory: A Life in the BBC*, London, 2003

Wyatt, Woodrow, *Confessions of an Optimist*, London, 1985

Wyndham Goldie, G., 'Viewing Television', *Listener*, 16 June 1937

— 'Television', in F. Laws (ed.), *Made for Millions*, London, 1947

— *Facing the Nation: Television and Politics 1936–1976*, London, 1977

Young, H., 'The Reality of the *Real Lives* Disaster', *Guardian*, 17 October 1985

Acknowledgements

To Alan Rusbridger, who commissioned this project and who edited the nine original newspaper articles from which this book sprang; my grateful thanks are due for his kind encouragement and rigorous guidance, and for the opportunity to undertake an assignment that at times seemed overwhelming, but was always fascinating.

To Laura Hassan of Guardian–Faber, who with grace and enthusiasm helped me shape the articles into a book, and to all the publishing team including Sara Montgomery, Jill Burrows and Anna Pallai.

To the many BBC staff and ex-staff who guided my understanding of the BBC and who gave me generous insights into their work; and to the many scholars of the BBC and observers of its workings who shared their views with me. I interviewed around a hundred people, some of whom spoke anonymously, others of whom are not quoted directly, but from all of whom I learned a great deal.

My thanks to the many friends and colleagues who offered support and wisdom, and to those who helped bring the original essays to the page: they include Michael Becker, Andy Beckett, Emily Bell, Chris Clarke, Alan Davey, Jon Day, Susanna Eastburn, Rupert Higgins, James Hislop, Paul Johnson, Paul Laity, Richard Nelsson, Andrew O'Hagan, Anne Perkins, Joshua St Johnston,

Fiona Shields, David Teather and Will Woodward. Particular thanks to Clare Margetson.

To Dan Sabbagh, who generously offered many insights gleaned from his former life as a media correspondent; and to the collective wisdom and generosity of the *Guardian*'s media reporting team.

To Professor Jean Seaton, official historian of the BBC, for her encouragement.

To Katie Ankers and her colleagues at the BBC Written Archives Centre. To the staff of the Rare Books & Music reading room at the British Library. To Laurie Klein of the Beinecke Library at Yale.

To Matthew Fox for the 'big stride of your mind' and for your love.

Georgina Henry died on 7 February 2014, aged fifty-three. She had been deputy editor of the *Guardian*, founded *Comment Is Free*, and, as head of culture, was, for a time, my boss. Earlier in her career she had been a fierce, strong and principled media editor. She was, to quote a description of Hilda Matheson, 'pure gold all the way through'. This book is dedicated, with love, to her memory.

Illustrations

Index

Page numbers in *italics* refer to photographs.

Index

Index

Index

Index